To my dear friend,
D. Mac Innes,
with best wishes
for Christmas.

J Brown.

MODERN
SCOTTISH POETRY

For
JOY

MODERN
SCOTTISH POETRY

An Anthology

of the Scottish Renaissance

1920–1945

edited by
MAURICE LINDSAY

FABER AND FABER LIMITED
24 Russell Square
London

First published in Mcmxlvi
by Faber and Faber Limited
24 Russell Square London W.C. 1
Printed in Great Britain by
R. MacLehose and Company Limited
The University Press Glasgow

CONTENTS

8

9

THE LITTLE WHITE ROSE

The Rose of all the world is not for me.
I want for my part
Only the little white rose of Scotland
That smells sharp and sweet—and breaks the heart.

HUGH MacDiarmid

ACKNOWLEDGMENTS

For permission to include copyright poems in this anthology I wish to thank the authors and publishers listed below: Violet Jacob, *Scottish Poems* (Oliver and Boyd); Pittendrigh MacGillivray, *Bog-Myrtle and Peet-Reek* (the late author and Miss MacGillivray); John Ferguson, *Thyrea* (Andrew Melrose [1927], Ltd. and Mrs. Ferguson); Marion Angus, *The Turn of the Day* (Faber and Faber); *Sun and Candlelight* (Faber and Faber); Helen B. Cruickshank, *Up the Noran Water* (Methuen); Hugh MacDiarmid, *Scots Unbound* (Aeneas MacKay); *Stony Limits* (Victor Gollancz); *Sangshaw* (Blackwood); *The Islands of Scotland* (Batsford); Alexander Gray, *Gossip* (Faber); *Songs and Ballads from Heine* (Grant Richards); Hamish MacLaren, *Sailor with Banjo* (Gollancz); Margot Robert Adamson, *Northern Holiday* (Cobden-Sanderson); Edwin Muir, *Journeys and Places* (Dent); *The Narrow Place* (Faber and Faber); Lewis Spence, *Plumes of Time* (Allen and Unwin); Andrew Young, *Collected Poems* (Cape); Muriel Stuart, *Poems* (Heineman); William Jeffrey, *Sea-Glimmer* (William Maclellan and Mrs. Jeffrey); William Soutar, *Collected Poems* (Andrew Dakers); Ruthven Todd, *The Acreage of the Heart* (William Maclellan); Robert Garioch, *Seventeen Poems for Sixpence* (The author); George Bruce, *Sea Talk* (William Maclellan); Douglas Young, *Auntran Blads* (William Maclellan); *A Braird o Thristles* (William Maclellan); J. F. Hendry, *The Bombed Happiness* (Routledge); Sorley Maclean, *Dain do Eimhir* (William Maclellan); Adam Drinan, *The Men on the Rocks* (Fortune Press); *The Ghosts of the Strath* (Fortune Press); G. S. Fraser, *Home Town Elegy* (PL. Nicholson and Watson); Norman McCaig, *Far Cry* (Routledge); Maurice Lindsay, *The Enemies of Love* (William Maclellan); W. S. Graham, *Cage without Grievance* (Parton Press); *2nd Poems* (PL. Nicholson and Watson); Sydney Smith, *The Deevil's Waltz* (William Maclellan); *The Wanderer and other Poems* (Oliver and Boyd), *Skail Wind* (The author);

13

I also wish to thank the editors and publishers of the following anthologies and periodicals for permission to publish poems which appeared within their pages: William Maclellan for poems by Hugh MacDiarmid, Edwin Muir, William Jeffrey, William Soutar, William Montgomerie, Sydney Smith, Adam Drinan, Robert MacLellan, Norman McCaig, Tom Scott, and Donald Macrae, which were published in my own *Poetry Scotland*; the editor of *Scottish Art and Letters* for poems by William Soutar, W. S. Graham and G. S. Fraser: the editors of *The White Horseman* (Routledge) for two poems by Tom Scott; the editor of *Life and Letters* for poems by J. F. Hendry, Maurice Lindsay and R. Crombie Saunders; the editor of *Modern Reading* for a poem by R. Crombie Saunders; the editor of *The New Alliance* for poems by Edwin Muir and the late Ann Scott-Moncrieff; the editor of *The Glasgow Evening News* for a poem by William Soutar; the editor of *Poetry Quarterly* for a poem by Ruthven Todd.

My thanks are due to the relatives of the late Donald Sinclair for the Gaelic text of *The Path of the Old Spells*. My special thanks to Hugh MacDiarmid and Douglas Young must be acknowledged —the former, for his Scots versions of poems by George Campbell Hay and Donald Sinclair, made for this volume: the latter for numerous kindnesses and helpful suggestions.

14

INTRODUCTION

When a literary movement of such energy and variety as the Scottish Renaissance comes certainly to flower, and grows and spreads over a period of twenty-five years, it is safe to assume that its roots run deep into the past. Those who are familiar with the surging courses of Scottish literature will themselves be able to trace the connections between the poems in this anthology and the work of earlier Scottish poets. But for many non-Scottish readers, a brief outline of the main influences which reflect upon the moderns may be helpful.

Without becoming involved in intricate ethnological argument, it is sufficient to say that, since the Middle Ages, two racial strains have gradually intermingled to form the Scottish character. The sturdy, tough-headed Lowlander has sprung mainly from Teuton stock, while the more romantic Western Highlander is Celtic in his origin.[1] To a great extent, Highlands and Lowlands have come together, and the division in modern Scotland is now largely a false one. Curiously enough, the gentler strain has predominated, and, for all his wiry practicality, the Lowland Scot carries the mournful blood of the Celt, which, when it comes to the surface, at once distinguishes him from his Northern English neighbour. It is this strange mixture of the racial factors which make up human personality that has resulted in the 'Caledonian antisyzygy', that warring of diverse elements as marked in Scottish literature as it is in the Scottish nature. The modern Scottish poet has the choice of at least two, and in some cases three, languages. And unless he can use them all with equal skill, his Scottish psyche must feel, in some degree, frustrated.

By the chance influences of environment and education, however, few Scots writers can handle Gaelic, Scots and English

[1] For a different, but not generally accepted view—that the Celtic influence is more marked in the Lowlands, and a Norse strain predominates in the Highlands—see Henderson's *Norse Influence in Celtic Scotland*.

with the same proficiency; and sooner or later each poet turns to the tongue in which he has acquired the most skill. But he is not debarred from reaping the fruits of a double literary heritage (I count the Scoto-English school together with the Scots, since space does not permit a detailed survey, since those who can understand the one can understand the other, and since both schools roughly exist in the same parts of the country). The Lowland group, with its roots in the sturdy Scots ballads of the Border country, embraces the work of the Makars—Henryson, Douglas, Dunbar and many others; the eighteenth century 'peasant' poets—Ramsay, Fergusson, and, of course, Burns; and the English-writing poets from Drummond of Hawthornden and James Thomson, to Scott and Byron. The Gaelic group has a tradition which stretches into the veiled mists of antiquity—for the Celt accompanies alike with his singing the great mysteries of birth and death and the daily domestic round—includes poems preserved in the Book of the Dean of Lismore, and that magnificent outburst of creative activity which went with, and followed, the luckless events of the 'Forty-Five'. For over six centuries[1] then, Scotland has nourished rich poetry in her three languages —to say nothing of the Latin poems composed in the first half of that period! But with the nineteenth century came a change.

For the art of poetry reached its nadir in Scotland during the nineteenth century. The first five decades brought to birth the publication *Whistlebinkie*, an amorphous collection wherein 'minor vernacular poets outdid each other in alternate laments and hiccoughs'; and from 1880 to 1897 a Mr. Edwards filled the sixteen volumes of his *Modern Scottish Poets* with unskilled and inconsequential pastiche. The nineteenth century worshipped what it conceived to be the spirit of Burns—the sentimental, moralising Rabbie who steered a plough between intervals of roistering drunkenness and energetic lovemaking. The 'immortal memory', toasted so solemnly every year, was but a cruel caricature of both the man and the poet. As a result, every homely versifier

---

[1] I have only taken account of written extant sources. The Ossianic lays, of course, stretch back to Roman times.

imitated the master, even to the point of borrowing his phrases and his lassies' names, whilst the 'educated' agreed with the worthy Dean Ramsay that the Scottish tongue was not a fit vehicle for the thoughts and expressions of cultured, mid-nineteenth century persons. So it happened that David Gray, the one original poet amongst them, who never forgot his Scottishness, writing to Lord Houghton in 1861, the last year of his brief life, complained that, if he used Scots, his work would 'fall dead from the presses'. There was always a market in Scotland for imitation Burns (and there still is!), but if a nineteenth century poet wanted an educated audience then he had to use English, and offer the polished flourishes of a Robert Buchanan.

Modern Scottish poetry really begins with Robert Louis Stevenson, John Davidson, and Andrew Lang. Davidson settled in London and eventually became an English poet and playwright. Stevenson and Lang wrote mostly in English—but English with distinctively Scottish flavour. There was a directness and sincerity altogether absent from the poems of, for instance, Dowson or Blunt. Celtic nostalgia was a predominant theme. There is nothing English in feeling about Lang's 'Almae Matres'—

> 'St. Andrews by the northern sea,
> A haunted town it is to me!
> A little city, worn and gray,
> The gray North Ocean girds it round;
> And o'er the rocks, and up the bay,
> The long sea-rollers surge and sound;
> And still the thin and biting spray
> Drives down the melancholy street,
> And still endure, and still decay,
> Towers that the salt winds vainly beat . . .'

or Stevenson in exile, longing for his native land—

> 'Be it granted to me to behold you again in dying,
> Hills of Home, and to hear again your call,
> Hear about the graves of the martyrs the peewees crying
> And hear no more at all!'

Lang and Stevenson were isolated Scotsmen moving across the English scene. And they would probably be surprised if they could look back now over the last fifty years and see how, unmistakably, they were the earliest writers who contributed to that resurgence of national poetry which has flowed, a continuous, widening stream, ever since. Charles Murray, their younger contemporary, employed a fuller canon of Scots than had been used since Burns wrote his Kilmarnock poems. Murray also made Scots 'respectable' again. But his work is of a light, half-humorous character, and save in a few pieces, he falls backwards into the depressing slough of nineteenth century sentimentality.

It was not until after the 1914–18 War that the Scottish Renaissance got fully under way. It was started as a deliberate search after national culture, a parallel to the political Scottish Nationalist movement, by C. M. Grieve (Hugh MacDiarmid) and Compton Mackenzie. The two volumes of *Northern Numbers* which appeared during the early 1920's contained, besides verse by the novelists John Buchan and Neil Munro, work by all the important poets and popular versifiers of the time, many of them now forgotten. It was only a beginning, as the editor, C. M. Grieve, stressed.

However, in all movements, it is the quality of the individuals' work which matters in the long run. The book which proved more of a stimulus to Scottish poets than anything else in their literature was Hugh MacDiarmid's *Sangshaw*, published in 1925. Here was a new strong Scots incorporating several local dialects, based on middle Scots, finished and turned on the wheel of adroit craftmanship: here were poems in Scots which contained *thought*, poems which strangely delighted and enriched the warp and woof of one's experience. It is largely under MacDiarmid's influence and through the inspiration of his remarkable personality that the younger poets, especially those who use Gaelic and Scots (or Lallans, as I prefer to call their Scots, drawing more, as it does, upon middle Scots) have developed. That influence is the spiritual urge to creativeness, and no mere slavish copying. Each of them is a highly personal artist.

18

Hugh MacDiarmid has written much, both in Scots and in English, but he has always held uncompromising views on the supreme place which Scots should occupy in future Scottish literature. He attacks Edwin Muir's erstwhile theory that Scottish poets would do well to throw away the Scottish tongue and concentrate upon writing in English, with considerable vigour and at great length in the introduction to his magnificent *Golden Treasury of Scottish Poetry*. The '*Golden Treasury*' goes up to about 1936, but although poems in English written during the previous centuries and the early years of this one are included, more recent work in English is not given a place.

Whether one likes it or not, the English language has come to stay in Scotland. It is absurd not to face up to this fact. But the work of many of those printed in *Modern Scottish Poetry* demonstrates that, whilst the words may be English, the poems of Scotsmen can still be wholeheartedly Scottish in texture and feeling. For many reasons English cannot and must not ever be allowed to supplant Scots. The two should exist side by side, as Gaelic and Scots have done for so many years. The Scots of MacDiarmid and the Lallans of Young and Smith can express nuances in Scottish life and thought which English could never do. The rich, resonant sounds of Scots are unique. On the other hand, it is less susceptible to the use of sensuous imagery, and continually menaced by the ease with which a careless diminutive can tumble it into a sticky morass of sentimentality. It cannot be too strongly stressed that Scots is an individual language derived not from Anglo-Saxon, but, in common with it, from an older Teutonic. Its modern version is no mere English provincial dialect. I cannot enter into the historical and etymological arguments here which would offer some proof of this assertion; but those who remain unconvinced and are disposed to pursue the matter further should refer to the essay, 'A Dissertation on the Origin of the Scottish Language', with which Dr. John Longmuir prefaces his edition of Jamieson's admirable *Dictionary of the Scottish Language*.

The poets in this anthology are arranged approximately in the order in which they first came before the public. Considerations of space made it quite impossible to go back to Stevenson, Davidson and Lang. Charles Murray is not included, partly because he belongs to the pre-Renaissance group, partly because his work, at its best, is witty, swift-moving verse excellent for its Scots rather than for poetic merit. I have also had to omit several 'one-piece' poets, and some Georgians, and others, whose work seems to me to have sadly dated: of the first, the most notable are Douglas Ainslie ('The Stirrup Cup'), Ronald Campbell MacFie ('In Memoriam: John Davidson'), and Will H. Ogilvie ('The Blades of Harden'). It was not without regret that I finally omitted Lord Alfred Douglas, Eric Linklater, George Reston Malloch, F. V. Branford and Sir William Watson. I cannot see that the Italianate poems of Rachel Annand Taylor qualify for inclusion in a Scottish anthology, despite their nominally Scottish subject-matter. The inclusion of Andrew Young I justify on the grounds that the poems by which he is represented show his early Scottish influences derived before he emigrated to an English village to become the most genial and delightful of modern English nature poets.

There may be many who will disagree with me on these and other points: no anthology can satisfy its every reader. My aim has been to make *Modern Scottish Poetry* a representative culling of the best fruits of the first twenty-five years of the Scottish Renaissance, with the bias, if any, in favour of the young. In time, I believe that most of these poems will pass into the corpus of permanent Scottish literature. Since many of the poets are still young, the anthology which covers the next quarter may do even better. But the work of the first quarter can stand comparison with the literature of any other European country over a similar period. It is certainly an encouraging portent for the new Scotland still struggling to be born.

MAURICE LINDSAY

20

VIOLET JACOB

THE WATER-HEN

As I gaed doon by the twa mill dams i' the mornin'
The water-hen cam' oot like a passin' wraith,
And her voice ran through the reeds wi' a sound of warnin',
        'Faith—keep faith!'
Aye, bird, tho' ye see but ane ye may cry on baith!'

As I gaed doon the field when the dew was lyin',
My ain love stood whaur the road an' the mill-lade met,
And it seemed to me that the rowin' wheel was cryin',
        'Forgi'e—forget,
And turn, man, turn, for ye ken that ye lo'e her yet!'

As I gaed doon the road 'twas a weary meetin',
For the ill words said yestreen they were aye the same,
And my het he'rt drouned the wheel wi' its heavy beatin'.
        'Lass, think shame,
It's no for me to speak, for it's you to blame!'

As I gaed doon by the toon when the day was springin'
The Baltic brigs lay thick by the soundin' quay
And the riggin' hummed wi' the sang that the wind was singin',
        'Free—gang free,
For there's mony a load on shore may be skailed at sea!'

When I cam hame wi' the thrang o' the years ahint me
There was naucht to see for the weeds and the lade in spate,
But the water-hen by the dam she seemed aye to mind me,
        Cryin' 'Hope—wait!'
'Aye, bird, but my een grow dim, an' it's late—late!'

TAM I' THE KIRK

O Jean, my Jean, when the bell ca's the congregation
   Owre valley an' hill wi' the ding frae its iron mou',
When a' body's thochts is set on his ain salvation,
      Mine's set on you.

There's a reid rose lies on the Buik o' the Word afore ye
   That was growin' braw on its bush at the keek o' day,
But the lad that pu'd yon flower i' the mornin's glory—
      He canna pray.

He canna pray; but there's nane i' the kirk will heed him
   Whar he sits sae still his lane by the side o' the wa',
For nane but the reid rose kens what my lassie gie'd him—
      It an' us twa!

He canna sing for the sang that his ain he'rt raises,
   He canna see for the mist that's afore his e'en,
And a voice drouns the hale o' the psalms an' the paraphrases,
      Cryin' 'Jean, Jean, Jean!'

THE NEEP-FIELDS BY THE SEA

Ye'd wonder foo the seasons rin
This side o' Tweed an' Tyne;
The hairst's awa'; October-month
Cam in a whilie syne,
But the stooks are oot in Scotland yet,
There's green upon the tree,
And oh! what grand's the smell ye'll get
Frae the neep-fields by the sea!

The lang lift lies abune the warld,
On ilka windless day
The ships creep doon the ocean line
Sma' on the band o' grey;

And the lang sigh heaved upon the sand
Comes pechin' up tae me
And speils the cliffs tae whaur ye stand
I' the neep-fields by the sea.

Oh, time's aye slow, tho' time gangs fast
When siller's a' tae mak',
An' deith, afore ma poke is fu'
May grip me i' the back;
But ye'll tak' ma banes an' my Sawbath braws,
Gin deith's ower smairt for me,
And set them up amang the shaws
I' the lang rows plantit atween the wa's,
A tattie-dulie for fleggin' craws
I' the neepfields by the sea.

THE WILD GEESE

'Oh, tell me what was on yer road, ye roarin' norlan' wind
As ye cam' blawin' frae the land that's niver frae my mind?
My feet they trayvel England, but I'm deein' for the north—'
'My man, I heard the siller tides rin up the Firth o' Forth.'

'Aye, Wind, I ken them well eneuch, and fine they fa' and rise,
And fain I'd feel the creepin' mist on yonder shore that lies,
But tell me, ere ye passed them by, what saw ye on the way?'
'My man, I rocked the rovin' gulls that sail abune the Tay.'

'But saw ye naethin', leein' Wind, afore ye cam' to Fife?
There's muckle lyin' yont the Tay that's mair to me nor life.'
'My man, I swept the Angus braes ye haena trod for years—'
'O Wind, forgie a hameless loon that canna see for tears!—'

'And far abune the Angus straths I saw the wild geese flee,
A lang, lang skein o' beatin' wings wi' their heids towards the sea,
And aye their cryin' voices trailed ahint them on the air—'
'O Wind, hae maircy, haud yer whisht, for I daurna listen mair!'

23

PITTENDRIGH MACGILLIVRAY

MERCY O' GODE

I

Twa bodachs, I mind, had a threep ae day,
        Aboot man's chief end—
        Aboot man's chief end.
Whan the t'ane lookit sweet his words war sour,
Whan the tither leuch out his words gied a clour,
But whilk got the better I wasna sure—
        I wasna sure,
        An' needna say.

II

But I mind them well for a queer-like pair—
        A gangrel kind,
        A gangrel kind:
The heid o' the ane was beld as an egg,
The ither, puir man, had a timmer leg,
An' baith for the bite could dae nocht but beg
        Nocht but beg—
        Or live on air!

III

On a table-stane in the auld Kirkyaird,
        They ca' 'The Houff',
        They ca' 'The Houff',
They sat in their rags like wearyfu' craws,
An' fankl't themsel's about a 'FIRST CAUSE',
An' the job the Lord had made o' His laws,
        Made o' his Laws,
        In human regaird.

IV

Twa broken auld men wi' little but jaw—
>> Faur better awa
>> Aye—better awa:
Yawmerin' owr things that nane can tell,
The yin for a Heaven, the ither for Hell;
Wi' nae mair in tune than a crackit bell—
>> A crackit bell,
>> Atween the twa.

V

Dour badly he barkit in praise o' the Lord—
>> 'The pooer o' Gode
>> An' the wull o' Gode';
But Stumpie believ't nor in Gode nor man—
Thocht life but a fecht without ony plan,
An' the best nae mair nor a flash i' the pan—
>> A flash i' the pan,
>> In darkness smored.

VI

Twa dune men—naither bite nor bed!—
>> A sair-like thing—
>> An' unco thing.
To the Houff they cam to lay their heid
An' seek a nicht's rest wi' the sleepin' deid,
Whar the stanes wudna grudge nor ony tak' heed
>> Nor ony tak' heed:
>> But it's ill to read.

VII

They may hae been bitter, an' dour, an' warsh,
>> But wha could blame—
>> Aye—wha could blame?
I kent bi their look they war no' that bad
But jist ill dune bi an' driven half mad:

25

Whar there's nae touch o' kindness this life's owr sad
     This life's owr sad,
      An' faur owr harsh.

VIII

But as nicht drave on I had needs tak' the road,
     Fell gled o' ma dog—
     The love o' a dog:
An' tho nane wad hae me that day at the fair,
I raither't the hill for a houff than in there,
'Neth a table-stane, on a deid man's lair—
     A deid man's lair—
      Mercy o' Gode.

GLANCES

O weel I mind the bonnie morn,
   Richt early in the day,
When he cam' in by oor toun end
   To buy a sou o' hay.

For O he was a handsome lad,
   An' weel did cock his beaver!—
He gar't my heart play pit-a-pat;
   Yet—speired but for my faither!

I turned aboot and gied a cast
   That plainly said—'Ye deevil!—
Altho' ye be a braw young lad
   Ye needna be unceevil!'

He glower't at me like ane gaen wud
   Wi' his daurin' rovin' een;
At that I leuch and wi' a fling
   Flew roun' the bourtree screen.

ABASSHYD

I toke hyr heid atween my hondes
 And kyste hyr dusky hair;
I lyghtly touchte hyr luvely cheek,
 Syn kyste hyr mouth so rare.

A lityll flame cam up hyr neck
 To tell hyr herte had fyre;
But, sum aschamte, wyth eyen cast down,
 Hyr mynde restrainte desyre.

A swete, pure mayde of gentyl kynd—
 A flowr ryght fayre to see:
Yet wyth ane potent gyfte of sowle
 Fro yll to keep hyr free.

Abasshte before hyr luvelyness
 I knelt and kyste hyr honde;
In token that I humbled me,
 And stayed at hyr commaunde.

JOHN FERGUSON

A COCK CROWING IN A POULTERER'S SHOP

He will not see the East catch fire again,
 Nor watch the darkening of the drowsy West,
 Nor sniff the morning air with joyous zest,
Nor lead his wives along the grassy lane.

27

Cooped in a crate, he claps his wings in vain,
   Then hangs his crimson head upon his breast;
   To-morrow's sun will see him plucked and dressed,
One of a ghastly row of feathered slain.

O chanticleer, I cannot bear it more;
   That crow of anguish, pitiful and stark,
      Makes my flesh quail at thy unhappy lot—
The selfsame cry with which thine ancestor
   Emptied his soul into the tragic dark
      The night that Peter said, 'I know Him not.'

MARION ANGUS

MARY'S SONG

I wad ha'e gi'en him my lips tae kiss,
Had I been his, had I been his;
Barley breid and elder wine,
Had I been his as he is mine.

The wanderin' bee it seeks the rose;
Tae the lochan's bosom the burnie goes;
The grey bird cries at evenin's fa',
'My luve, my fair one, come awa'.'

My beloved sall ha'e this he'rt tae break,
Reid, reid wine and the barley cake,
A he'rt tae break, and a mou' tae kiss,
Tho' he be nae mine, as I am his.

ALAS! POOR QUEEN

She was skilled in music and the dance
And the old arts of love
At the court of the poisoned rose
And the perfumed glove,
And gave her beautiful hand
To the pale Dauphin
A triple crown to win—
And she loved little dogs
         And parrots
      And red-legged partridges
And the golden fishes of the Duc de Guise
And a pigeon with a blue ruff
She had from Monsieur d'Elbœuf.

Master John Knox was no friend to her;
She spoke him soft and kind,
Her honeyed words were Satan's lure
The unwary soul to bind.
'Good sir, doth a lissome shape
And a comely face
Offend your God His Grace
Whose Wisdom maketh these
Golden fishes of the Duc de Guise?'

She rode through Liddesdale with a song;
'Ye streams sae wondrous strang,
Oh, mak' me a wrack as I come back
But spare me as I gang.'
While a hill-bird cried and cried
Like a spirit lost
By the grey storm-wind tost.

Consider the way she had to go.
Think of the hungry snare,
The net she herself had woven,
Aware or unaware,
Of the dancing feet grown still,
The blinded eyes—
Queens should be cold and wise,
And she loved little things,
            Parrots
        And red-legged partridges
And the golden fishes of the Duc de Guise
And the pigeon with the blue ruff
She had from Monsieur d'Elbœuf.

THINK LANG

Lassie, think lang, think lang,
Ere his step comes ower the hill.
Luve gi'es wi' a lauch an' a sang,
An' whiles for nocht but ill.

Thir's weary time tae rue
In the lea-lang nicht yer lane
The ghaist o' a kiss on yer mou'
An' sough o' win' in the rain.

Lassie, think lang, think lang,
The trees is clappin' their han's,
The burnie clatterin' wi' sang
Rins ower the blossomy lan's.

Luve gi'es wi' a lauch an' a sang,
His fit fa's licht on the dew.
Oh, lass, are ye thinkin' lang,
Star een an' honey mou'?

THE LILT

Jean Gordon is weaving a' her lane
Twinin' the threid wi' a thocht o' her ain,
Hearin' the tune o' the bairns at play
That they're singin' amang them ilka day;
And saftly, saftly, ower the hill
Comes the sma', sma' rain.

Aye, she minds o' a simmer's nicht
Afore the waning o' the licht—
Bairnies chantin' in Lover's lane
The sang that comes ower and ower again,
And a young lass stealin' awa' to the hill,
In the sma', sma' rain.

Oh! lass, your lips were flamin' reid,
An' cauld, mist drops lay on yer' heid,
Ye didna gaither yon rose yer' lane
And yer' hert was singin' a sang o' its ain,
As ye slippit hameward, ower the hill,
In the sma', sma' rain.

Jean Gordon, she minds as she sits her lane
O' a' the years that's bye and gane,
And naething gi'en and a' thing ta'en
But yon nicht o' nichts on the smoory hill
In the sma', sma' rain—
And the bairns are singin' at their play
The lilt that they're liltin' ilka day.

HELEN B. CRUICKSHANK

SHY GEORDIE

Up the Noran Water,
In by Inglismaddy,
Annie's got a bairnie
That hasna got a daddy.
Some say it's Tammas's
And some say it's Chay's;
An' naebody expec'it it,
Wi' Annie's quiet ways.

Up the Noran Water,
The bonnie little mannie
Is dandlit an' cuddlit close
By Inglismaddy's Annie.
Wha the bairnie's faither is
The lassie never says;
But some think it's Tammas's,
And some think it's Chay's.

Up the Noran Water
The country folk are kind;
An' wha the bairnie's daddy is
They dinna muckle mind.
But oh! the bairn at Annie's breist,
The love in Annie's e'e!
They mak' me wish wi' a' my micht
The lucky lad was me!

HUGH MACDIARMID

THE BONNIE BROUKIT BAIRN

(For Peggy)

Mars is braw in crammasy,
Venus in a green silk goun,
The auld mune shak's her gowden feathers,
Their starry talk's a wheen o' blethers,
Nane for thee a thochtie sparin',
Earth, thou bonnie broukit bairn!
—But greet, an' in your tears ye'll droun
The haill clanjamfrie!

MILK-WORT AND BOG-COTTON

Cwa' een like milk-wort and bog-cotton hair!
I love you, earth, in this mood best o' a'
When the shy spirit like a laich wind moves
And frae the lift nae shadow can fa'
Since there's nocht left to thraw a shadow there
Owre een like milk-wort and milk-white cotton hair.

Wad that nae leaf upon anither wheeled
A shadow either and nae root need dern
In sacrifice to let sic beauty be!
But deep surroondin' darkness I discern
Is aye the price o' licht. Wad licht revealed
Naething but you, and nicht nocht else concealed.

WITH THE HERRING FISHERS

'I see herrin'.'—I hear the glad cry
And 'gainst the moon see ilka blue jowl
In turn as the fishermen haul on the nets
And sing: 'Come, shove in your heids and growl.'

'Soom on, bonnie herrin', soom on,' they shout,
Or 'Come in, O come in, and see me',
'Come gie the auld man something to dae.
It'll be a braw change frae the sea.'

O it's ane o' the bonniest sichts in the warld
To watch the herrin' come walkin' on board
In the wee sma' 'oors o' a simmer's mornin'
As if o' their ain accord.

For this is the way that God sees life,
The haill jing-bang o's appearin'
Up owre frae the edge o' naethingness
—It's his happy cries I'm hearin'.

'Left, right—O come in and see me,'
Reid and yellow and black and white
Toddlin' up into Heaven thegither
At peep o' day frae the endless night.

'I see herrin',' I hear his glad cry,
And 'gainst the moon see his muckle blue jowl,
As he handles buoy-tow and bush raip
Singin': 'Come, shove in your heids and growl!'

THE WATERGAW

Ae weet forenicht i' the yow-trummle
I saw yon antrin thing,
A watergaw wi' its chitterin' licht
Ayont the on-ding;
An' I thocht o' the last wild look ye gied
Afore ye dee'd!

There was nae reek i' the laverock's hoose
That nicht—an' nane i' mine;
But I hae thocht o' that foolish licht
Ever sin' syne;
An' I think that mebbe at last I ken
What your look meant then.

OF JOHN DAVIDSON

I remember one death in my boyhood
That next to my father's, and darker, endures;
Not Queen Victoria's, but Davidson, yours,
And something in me has always stood
Since then looking down the sandslope
On your small black shape by the edge of the sea,
—A bullet-hole through a great scene's beauty,
God through the wrong end of a telescope.

from
SECOND HYMN TO LENIN

Oh, it's nonsense, nonsense,
Nonsense at this time o' day
That breid-and-butter problems
S'ud be in ony man's way.

They su'd be like the tails we tint
On leaving the monkey stage;
A' maist folk fash aboot's alike
Primaeval to oor age.

We're grown-up folk that haena yet
Put bairnly things aside
—A' that's material and moral—
And oor new state descried.

Sport, love, and parentage,
Trade, politics, and law
S'ud be nae mair to us than braith
We hardly ken we draw.

Freein' oor poo'ers for greater things,
And feg's there's plenty o' them,
Tho' wha's still trammelt in alow
Canna be tenty o' them—

IN THE FOGGY TWILIGHT

I lay in the foggy twilight
In a hollow o' the hills and saw
Moisture getherin' slowly on the heather cowes
In drops no' quite heavy eneuch to fa'.

And I kent I was still like that
Wi' the spirit o' God, alas!;
Lyin' in wait in vain for a single grey grey drop
To quicken into perfect quidditas.

PERFECT

(On the Western Seaboard of Uist)
Los muertos los ojos a los que viven

I found a pigeon's skull on the machair,
All the bones pure white and dry, and chalky,
But perfect,
Without a crack or a flaw anywhere.

At the back, rising out of the beak,
Were twin domes like bubbles of thin bone,
Almost transparent, where the brain had been
That fixed the tilt of the wings.

TWO MEMORIES

Religion? Huh! Whenever I hear the word
It brings two memories back to my mind.
Choose between them and tell me which
You think the better model for mankind.

Fresh blood scares sleeping cows worse than anything else on
    earth.
An unseen rider leans far out from his horse with a freshly-
    skinned
Weaner's hide in his hands, turning and twisting the hairy slimy
    thing
And throwing the blood abroad on the wind.

A brilliant flash of lightning crashes into the heavens.
It reveals the earth in a strange yellow-green light,
Alluring yet repelling, that distorts the immediate foreground
And makes the gray and remote distance odious to the sight.

And a great mass of wraithlike objects on the bed ground
Seems to upheave, to move, to rise, to fold and undulate
In a wavelike mobility that extends to an alarming distance.
The cows have ceased to rest: they are getting to their feet.

Another flash of lightning shows a fantastic and fearsome vision.
Like the branches of some enormous grotesque sprawling plant
A forest of long horns waves, and countless faces
Turn into the air, unspeakably weird and gaunt.

The stroke of white fire is reflected back
To the heavens from thousands of bulging eyeballs,
And into the heart of any man who sees
This diabolical mirroring of the lightning numbing fear falls.

Is such a stampede your idea for the human race?
Haven't we milled in it long enough? My second memory
Is of a flight of wild swans. Glorious white birds in the blue
    October heights
Over the surly unrest of the ocean! Their passing is more than
    music to me
And from their wings descends, and in my heart triumphantly
    peals
The old loveliness of earth that both affirms and heals.

ALEXANDER GRAY

SCOTLAND

Here in the uplands
The soil is ungrateful;
The fields, red with sorrel,
Are stony and bare.

38

A few trees, wind-twisted—
Or are they but bushes?—
Stand stubbornly guarding
A home here and there.

Scooped out like a saucer,
The land lies before me,
The waters, once scattered,
Flow orderly now
Through fields where the ghosts
Of the marsh and the moorland
Still ride the old marches,
Despising the plough.

The marsh and the moorland
Are not to be banished;
The bracken and heather,
The glory of broom,
Usurp all the balks
And the fields' broken fringes,
And claim from the sower
Their portion of room.

This is my country,
The land that begat me.
These windy spaces
Are surely my own,
And those who here toil
In the sweat of their faces
Are flesh of my flesh
And bone of my bone.

Hard is the day's task—
Scotland, stern Mother!—
Wherewith at all times
Thy sons have been faced—

Labour by day,
And scant rest in the gloaming,
With want an attendant
Not lightly outpaced.

Yet do thy children
Honour and love thee,
Harsh is thy schooling
Yet great is the gain.
True hearts and strong limbs,
The beauty of faces
Kissed by the wind
And caressed by the rain.

HEINE IN SCOTS

There were three kings cam' frae the East;
They spiered in ilka clachan:
'O, which is the wey to Bethlehem,
My bairns, sae bonnily lachin'?'

O neither young nor auld could tell;
They trailed till their feet were weary.
They followed a bonny gowden starn,
That shone in the lift sae cheery.

The starn stüde ower the ale-hoose byre
Whaur the stable gear was hingin'.
The owsen mooed, the bairnie grat,
The kings begoud their singin'.

GRIEF

What ails you, you puir auld body?
    What gars you greet sae sair?
Hae you tint the man that's been kind to you
    This forty year and mair?

O, I didna greet when I tint him,
  Nor yet on the burrel-day;
But though I saw to the horse and byre,
  God kens that my hert was wae.

But this mornin' I cam on his bauchles;
  What cud I dae but greet?
For I mindit hoo hard he had wrocht for me,
  Trauchlin' wi' sair, sair feet.

FLOTSAM

When I see a man suffering and hungry and cold,
  In gaping rags selling his wares in the street;
Counting the scanty pence for the trash he has sold;
  Chafing his hands, shuffling his frozen feet;

Passing, I look in the dulled eyes, once so keen;
  And I see, though I would not, the hands which the years have
    defiled,
And the unkempt, matted beard, tangled, unclean,
  And the mouth that was once the pouting mouth of a child.

And always I think of the woman who, years before,
  In her fruitful youth was glad in Love's rapturous fire,
Who, faring alone in the valley of suffering, bore
  A son, the seal of her own and her lover's desire.

And she was proud in the joy of her motherhood,
  Pitying other women denied her bliss,
And she gave all, and found that giving was good,
  Gave in the end to the world which has made of him—this.

These are the feet which once, in devotion, she kissed,
  Counting again and again the delicate toes;
And she fondled the fold of flesh round the baby wrist,
  And the flawlessly fashioned ears and the tiny nose.

41

Mothers of men, for a few swift seasons you may
    Shepherd and shield and shelter the child of your care!
It is well that your eyes may not see the stony way
    Down which the feet you now kiss may one day fare.

HAMISH MACLAREN

ISLAND ROSE

She has given all her beauty to the water;
    She has told her secrets to the tidal bell;
And her hair is a moon-drawn net, and it has caught her,
    And her voice is in the hollow shell.

She will not come back any more now, nor waken
    Out of her island dream where no wind blows:
And only in the small house of the shell, forsaken,
    Sings the dark one whose face is a rose.

ALBERT D. MACKIE

MOLECATCHER

Strampin' the bent, like the Angel o' Daith,
    The mowdie-man staves by;
Alang his pad the mowdie-worps
    Like sma' Assyrians lie.

42

And where the Angel o' Daith has been,
    Yirked oot o' their yirdy hames,
Lie Sennacherib's blasted hosts
    Wi' guts dung oot o' wames.

Sma' black tramorts wi' gruntles grey,
    Sma' weak weemin's han's,
Sma' bead-een that wid touch ilk hert
    Binnae the mowdie-man's.

MARGOT ROBERT ADAMSON

EDINBURGH

If they should ask what makes the stuff of us
We should call up such idle things and gone!
The theatre we knew in Grindley Street,
The midnight bell vibrating in the Tron.

A church tower's clock along the Lothian Road,
Whose face lit up would turn a lemon moon,
Seen o'er the pallid bleakness of the street
In the chill dusks that harry northern June,

A Sunday morning over Samson's Ribs,
The smoky grass that grows on Arthur's Seat;
Turned-yellow willow leaves in Dalkeith Road,
Dropt lanceheads on the pavement at our feet;

Glimpses got sometimes of the Forfar hills
With the white snows upon them, or, maybe,
Green waters washing round the piers of Leith
With all the straws and flotsam of the sea.

A certain railway bridge whence one can look
On a network of bright lines and feel the stress,
Tossing its plumes of milky snow, where goes
Loud in full pace the thundering North Express

Behind its great green engine; or in Spring
Black-heaved the Castle Rock and there where blows
By Gordon's window wild the wallflower still,
The gold that keeps the footprints of Montrose.

The Pentlands over yellow stubble fields
Seen out beyond Craigmillar, and the flight
Of seagulls wheeling round the dark-shared plough,
Strewing the landscape with a rush of white.

Such idle things! Gold birches by hill lochs,
The gales that beat the Lothian shores in strife,
The day you found the great blue alkanette,
And all the farmlands by the shores of Fife.

DONALD SINCLAIR

SLIGH NAN SEANN SEUN

Saoibhir sith nan sian an nochd air Tìr-an-Àigh.
Is ciùine ciuil nam fiath ag iadhadh Innse Gràidh,
Is èasgaidh gach sgiath air fianlach dian an Dàin
Is slighe nan seann seun a' siaradh siar gun tàmh.
Saoibhir com nan cruach le cuimhne làithean aosd',
Sona gnuis nan cuan am bruadair uair a dh' aom;
Soillseach gach uair an aigne suaimhneach ghaoth—
O, làithean mo luaidh, 'ur n-uaill, 'ur uails', 'ur gaol!

O, làithean geala gràidh le'r gnàthan geala còir',
O, aimsirean an 'aigh le'r gàire, gean, is ceòl—
O, shaoghail nan gràs nan gàthan aithne 's eòil,
C'uime thréig 's nach d' fhàg ach àilte àin 'ur glòir?
An ioghnadh deòin is dùil bhi dol an null 'nur déidh,
Ri ionndruinn nan rùn a lion 'ur sgùird le spéis?
An ioghnadh ceòl nan dùl bhi seinn air cliù 'ur réim'
Is fabhra crom gach sùl' bhi tais fo dhùbhradh leug?
A làithean sin a thriall le ial-luchd àis mo shluaigh,
C'uime thàrr 'ur miann gach dias a b'fhiachmhor buaidh?
An ioghnadh an iarmailt shiar bhi nochd fo shnuadh,
'S'ur n-àrosan an cian bhi laist le lias bith-bhuan?
An ioghnadh lom gach làir bhi luaidh air làn 'ur sgeòil?
An ioghnadh cnuic is ràdh a' chomha-thràth 'nam beòil?
An ioghnadh cruit nan dàn bhi bìth fo sgàil' a neòil—
Is ealaidh-ghuth nam bàrd gun seun, gun sàire seoil?
Chan ioghnadh cill mo shluaigh an cois nan cuan bhi balbh,
Chan ioghnadh uchd nan tuam bhi'n tòic le luach na dh' fhalbh,
O, shaoghail, is truagh nach till aon uair a shearg,
'S nach tàrr mo dheòin, ge buan, aon fhios á suain nam marbh!

THE PATH OF THE OLD SPELLS
from the Gaelic of Donald Sinclair
(*Scots version by Hugh MacDiarmid*)

Rich is the peace o' the elements the nicht owre the Land o' Joy
And rich the evenness o' the calm's music roond the Isles o' Love,
Ilka wing plies urgently in obedience to nature
While the path o' the auld spells winds inexorably westwards.
Rich the breist o' the hills wi' memories o' bygone days,
Serene the face o' the seas wi' dreams o' the times that are gane.
O seilfu' days, your pride, your nobleness, your love!
O white days o' love wi' your clean and kindly ways!
O times o' joy wi' your lauchter, your cheer, and your music!
O warld o' grace, lit by rays o' knowledge and art!

Why ha'e you gane and left hardly a trace
   o' the noontide o' your glory?
Is it a wonder desire and hope seek to follow eftir you,
Fain for the secrets that aince cled your lap wi' esteem?
Is it a wonder the elements sing o' your time and poo'er
And the curved lid o' ilka eye is weak frae the fire o' jewels?
O yon days that ha'e gane wi' the shinin' load o' the wisdom o'
   my race,
Why did you want to strip awa' ilka last ear o' maist worthy
   excellence?
Nae wonder the western lift is noo sae illustrious wi' licht
And that your dwellin's in the distance are alowe wi' an ever-
   lastin' flame!
Nae wonder the bareness o' ilka flat bespeaks the fullness o' your
   story!
Nae wonder the hills haud the words o' twilicht in their mooths!
Nae wonder the harp o'the sangs is silent under the belly o' yon
   clood
And the voice-of-song o' the bards without spell or excellence o'
   art!
Nae wonder the kirkyaird o' my folk, by the sea, is dumb!
Nae wonder the breists o' the graves are a' hoven wi' the worth o'
   what's gane!
O Warld! It is a woe that no' an 'oor that has gane can ever come
   back,
Nor can my desire, tho' lastin', draw a single word frae the sleep
   o' the deid!

EDWIN MUIR

ROBERT THE BRUCE STRICKEN
WITH LEPROSY: TO DOUGLAS

'My life is done, yet all remains,
    The breath has vanished, the image not,
The furious shapes once forged in heat
    Live on, though now no longer hot.

'Steadily the shining swords
    In order rise, in order fall,
In order on the beaten field
    The faithful trumpets call.

'The women weeping for the dead
    Now are not sad but dutiful,
The dead men stiffening in their place
    Proclaim the ancient rule.

'Great Wallace's body hewn in four,
    So altered, stays as it must be.
O Douglas, do not leave me now,
    For by your side I see

'My dagger sheathed in Comyn's heart,
    And nothing there to praise or blame,
Nothing but order which must be
    Itself and still the same.

'But that Christ hung upon the Cross,
    Comyn would rot until Time's end
And bury my sin in boundless dust,
    For there is no amend.

'In order; yet in order run
    All things by unreturning ways.
If Christ live not, nothing is there
    For sorrow or for praise.'

So the King spoke to Douglas once
    A little time before his death,
Having outfaced three English kings
    And kept a people's faith.

MARY STUART

My brother Jamie lost me all,
Fell cleverly to make me fall,
And with a sure reluctant hand
Stole my life and took my land.

It was jealousy of the womb
That let me in and shut him out,
Honesty, kingship, all shut out,
While I enjoyed the royal room.

My father was his, but not my mother,
We were, yet were not, sister, brother,
To reach my mother he had to strike
Me down and leap that deadly dyke.

Over the wall I watched him move
At ease through all the guarded grove,
Then hack, and hack, and hack it down,
Until that ruin was his own.

48

SCOTLAND, 1941

We were a family, a tribe, a people,
Wallace and Bruce guard now a painted field,
And all may read the folio of our fable,
Peruse the sword, the sceptre and the shield.
A simple sky roofed in that rustic day,
The busy corn-fields and the haunted holms,
The green path winding up the ferny brae.
But Knox and Melville clapped their preaching palms
And huddled all the harvest gold away,
Hoodicrow Peden in the blighted corn
Hacked with his rusty beak the starving haulms.
Out of that desolation we were born.

Courage beyond the point and obdurate pride
Gave us a nation, robbed us of a nation.
Defiance absolute and myriad-eyed
That could not pluck the palm plucked our damnation.
We with such courage and the bitter wit
To fell the ancient oak of loyalty,
And strip the peopled hill and the altar bare,
And crush the poet with an iron text,
How could we read our souls and learn to be?

A pallid drove of faces harsh and vexed,
We watch our cities burning in their pit,
To salve our souls grinding dull lucre out,
We, fanatics of the frustrate and the half,
Who once set Purgatory Hill in doubt.
Now smoke and dearth and money everywhere,
Grim heirlooms of each fainter generation,
And mummied housegods in their musty niches,
Burns and Scott, sham bards of a sham nation,
And spiritual defeat wrapped warm in riches,

No pride but pride of pelf. Long since the young
Died in great bloody battles to carve out
This towering pulpit of the Golden Calf.
Montrose, Mackail, Argyll, perverse and brave,
Twisted the stream, unhooped the ancestral hill.
Never had Dee or Don or Yarrow or Till
Huddled such thriftless honour in a grave.

If we could raise those bones so brave and wrong,
Revive our ancient body, part by part.
We'd touch to pity the annalist's iron tongue
And gather a nation in our sorrowful heart.

THEN

There were no men and women then at all,
But bone grinding on bone,
And angry shadows fighting on a wall
That now and then sent out a groan
Mingled with lime and stone,
And sweated now and then like tortured wood
Big drops that looked yet did not look like blood.

And yet as each drop came a shadow faded
And left the wall.
There was a lull
Until another in its shadow arrayed it,
Came, fought and left a blood-mark on the wall.
And that was all: the blood was all.

If women had been there they would have wept
To see the blood, unowned, unwanted,
Poor as forgotten script.
The wall was haunted
By mute maternal presences whose sighing
Fluttered the fighting shadows and shook the wall
As if that fury of death itself were dying.

50

THE SUFFICIENT PLACE

See, all the silver roads wind in, lead in
To this still place like evening. See, they come
Like messengers bearing gifts to this little house,
And this great hill worn down to a patient mound,
And these tall trees whose motionless branches bear
An aeon's summer foliage, leaves so thick
They seem to have robbed a world of shade, and kept
No room for all these birds that line the boughs
With heavier riches, leaf and bird and leaf.
Within the doorway stand
Two figures, Man and Woman, simple and clear
As a child's first images. Their manners are
Such as were known before the earliest fashion
Taught the Heavens guile. The room inside is like
A thought that needed thus much space to write on,
Thus much, no more. Here all's sufficient. None
That comes complains, and all the world comes here,
Comes, and goes out again, and comes again.
This is the Pattern, these the Prototypes,
Sufficient, strong and peaceful. All outside
From end to end of the world is tumult. Yet
These roads do not turn in here but writhe on
Round the wild earth for ever. If a man
Should chance to find this place three times in Time
His eyes are changed and make a summer silence
Amid the tumult, seeing the roads wind in
To their still home, the house and the leaves and birds.

THE LITTLE GENERAL

Early in spring the little General came
Across the sound, bringing the island death,
And suddenly a place without a name,
And like the pious ritual of a faith,

Hunter and quarry in the boundless trap,
The white smoke curling from the silver gun,
The feather curling in the hunter's cap,
And clouds of feathers floating in the sun,

While down the birds came in a deafening shower,
Wing-hurricane, and the cattle fled in fear,
Up on the hill a remnant of a tower
Had watched that single scene for many a year,

Weaving a wordless tale where all were gathered
(Hunter and quarry and watcher and fabulous field),
A sylvan war half human and half feathered,
Perennial emblem painted on the shield

Held up to cow a never-conquered land
Fast in the little General's fragile hand.

LEWIS SPENCE

THE QUEEN'S BATH-HOUSE, HOLYROOD

Time that has dinged doun castels and hie toures,
And cast great crouns like tinsel in the fire,
That halds his hand for palace nor for byre,
Stands sweir at this, the oe of Venus' boures.
Not Time himself can dwall withouten floures,
Though aiks maun fa' the rose sall bide entire;
So sall this diamant of a queen's desire
Outflourish all the stanes that Time devours.

Mony a strength his turret-heid sall tine
Ere this sall fa' whare a queen lay in wine,
Whose lamp was her ain lily flesh and star.
The walls of luve the mair triumphant are
Gif luve were waesome habiting that place;
Luve has maist years that has a murning face.

PORTRAIT OF MARY STUART, HOLYROOD

Wauken be nicht, and bydand on some boon,
  Glamour of saul, or spirituall grace,
  I haf seen sancts and angells in the face,
And like a fere of seraphy the moon;
But in nae mirk nor sun-apparelled noon
  Nor pleasance of the planets in their place
  Of luve devine haf seen sae pure a trace
As in yon shadow of the Scottis croun.

Die not, O rose, dispitefull of hir mouth,
  Nor be ye lillies waeful at hir snaw;
    This dim devyce is but hir painted sake,
The mirour of ane star of vivand youth,
    That not hir velvets nor hir balas braw
      Can oueradorn, or luve mair luvely make.

ANDREW YOUNG

LOCH BRANDY

All day I heard the water talk
From dripping rock to rock
And water in bright snowflakes scatter
On boulders of the black Whitewater;
But louder now than these
The silent scream of the loose tumbling screes.

Grey wave on grey stone hits
And grey moth flits
Moth after moth, but oh,
What floats into that silver glow,
What golden moth
That rises with a strange majestic sloth?

O heart, why tremble with desire
As on the water shakes that bridge of fire?
The gold moth floats away, too soon
To narrow to a hard white moon
That scarce will light the path
Stumbling to where the cold mist wreaths the **strath**.

THE MOUNTAIN

The burn ran blacker for the snow
And ice-floe on ice-floe
Jangled in heavy lurches
Beneath the claret-coloured birches.

Dark grouse rose becking from the ground
And deer turned sharp heads round,
The antlers on their brows
Like stunted trees with withered boughs.

I climbed to where the mountain sloped
And long wan bubbles groped
Under the ice's cover,
A bridge that groaned as I crossed over.

I reached the mist, brighter than day,
That showed a specious way
By narrow crumbling shelves,
Where rocks grew larger than themselves.

But when I saw the mountain's spire
Looming through that damp fire,
I left it still unwon
And climbed down to the setting sun.

THE PAPS OF JURA

Before I crossed the sound
    I saw how from the sea
These breasts rise soft and round,
    Not two but three;

Now, climbing, I clasp rocks
    Storm-shattered and sharp-edged,
Grey ptarmigan their flocks,
    With starved moss wedged;

And mist like hair hangs over
    One barren breast and me,
Who climb, a desperate lover,
    With hand and knee.

THE ECHOING CLIFF

White gulls that sit and float,
Each on his shadow like a boat,
Sandpipers, oystercatchers
And herons, those grey stilted watchers,
From loch and corran rise,
And as they scream and squawk abuse
Echo from wooded cliff replies
So clearly that the dark pine boughs,
Where goldcrests flit
And owls in drowsy wisdom sit,
Are filled with sea-birds and their cries.

MURIEL STEWART

THE SEED SHOP

Here in a quiet and dusty room they lie,
  Faded as crumbled stone or shifting sand,
Forlorn as ashes, shrivelled, scentless, dry,
  Meadows and gardens running through my hand.

Dead that shall quicken at the trump of Spring,
  Sleepers to stir beneath June's splendid kiss,
Though birds pass over, unremembering,
  And no bee seek here roses that were his.

In this brown husk a dale of hawthorn dreams,
  A cedar in this narrow cell is thrust
That will drink deeply of a century's streams;
  These lilies shall make Summer on my dust.

Here in their safe and simple house of death,
    Sealed in their shells a million roses leap;
Here I can blow a garden with my breath,
    And in my hand a forest lies asleep.

THE WOOD AND THE SHORE

The low bay melts into a ring of silver,
And slips it on the shore's reluctant finger.
Though in an hour the tide will turn, will tremble,
Forsaking her because the moon persuades him.
But the black wood that leans and sighs above her
No hour can change, no moon can slave or summon.
Then comes the dark; on sleepy, shell-strewn beaches,
O'er long, pale leagues of sand, and cold clear water
She hears the tide go out towards the moonlight.
The wood still leans ... weeping she turns to seek him
And his black hair all night is on her bosom.

IN THE ORCHARD

'I thought you loved me.'
                        'No, it was only fun.'
'When we stood there, closer than all?'
                             'Well, the harvest moon
Was shining and queer in your hair, and it turned my head.'
'That made you?'
             'Yes.'
                   'Just the moon and the light it made
Under the tree?'
                      'Well, your mouth too.'
                           'Yes. My mouth?'

57

'And the quiet there that sang like the drum in the booth.
You shouldn't have danced like that.'

'Like what?'

'So close,
With your head turned up, and the flower in your hair, a rose
That smelt all warm.'

'I loved you. I thought you knew
I wouldn't have danced like that with any but you.'
'I didn't know. I thought you knew it was fun.'
'I thought it was love you meant.'

'Well, it's done.'

'Yes, it's done.
I've seen boys stone a blackbird, and watched them drown
A kitten . . . it clawed at the reeds, and they pushed it down
Into the pool while it screamed. Is that fun, too?'
'Well, boys are like that . . . your brothers . . .'

'Yes, I know.
But you, so lovely and strong! Not you! Not you!'
'They don't understand it's cruel. It's only a game.'
'And are girls fun, too?'

'No. Still in a way it's the same.
It's queer and lovely to have a girl . . .'

'Go on.'

'It makes you mad for a bit to feel she's your own,
And you laugh and kiss her, and maybe you give her a ring,
But it's only in fun.'

'But I gave you everything.'

'Well, you shouldn't have done it. You know what a fellow thinks
When a girl does that.'

'Yes, talks of her over his drinks
And calls her a ———"

'Stop that now. I thought you knew.'

'But it wasn't with anyone else. It was only you.'
'How did I know? I thought you wanted it too.
I thought you were like the rest—Well, what's to be done?'
'To be done?'

58

'Is it all right?'

'Yes.'

'Sure?'

'Yes, but why?'

'I don't know. I thought you were going to cry.
You said you had something to tell me.'

'Yes, I know.
It wasn't anything really . . . I think I'll go.'
'Yes, it's late. There's thunder about, a drop of rain
Fell on my hand in the dark. I'll see you again
At the dance next week. You're sure that everything's right?'
'Yes.'

'Well, I'll be going.'

'Kiss me . . .'

'Good night . . .'

'Good night.'

WILLIAM JEFFREY

IN MIDMOST WINTER

In midmost winter, when the wild Atlantic
Sends streams of cloud mast-high across the land
And ambient dark is matched by inner darkness—
The nations having bloody wars on hand—
In search of succour for my tortured spirit,
Such images as might transpose its woe
(For daily violence tears the roots of being)
    I take the road that twines
    In ample curves and lines
Where Tinto breasts the sky and clear Clyde waters flow.

The sequent motion of mechanic footsteps,
And tingling wrestle with the stormy wind
Prepare my senses for receptive quiet
And plant expectancy within my mind.
The scene familiar—quilted base of Tinto,
Thankerton common, browsing fleece of sheep,
Heathland of the muircock, covert of the pigeon—
    Transform in subtle change
    To woods where past times range,
And the dead in gray assemblies silent vigil keep.

Three shades I notice; soldiers of the eagle
Who heard the Tiber and the Rhone in flood,
Whose gaze enfolds the fall of church and city,
And Caesar on the stones, aflame in blood;
And three I see—shades that fought with Wallace
And shaped their lips on Barbour's noble cry;
And shades that with the stubborn Covenanters
    Kept watch in heath and ling
    Under the curlew's wing,
While the impassioned psalms rolled up into the sky

As I proceed within the ash-grey woodland,
Whose substance is of insubstantial glass,
The glances of the dead focus behind me
And follow tense and wheel-like as I pass.
Wherefore the rapt and gelid-burning glances?
What gazebo follows my unsilenced feet?
In solemn cohorts, all the slain in battle
    Gather behind me there,
    Crowding the vacant air
With sheen as of cotton flower that flutters over peat.

Then murmur of inward voices—'Oh, Clyde waters,
Clyde waters gently flowing' I heard them say—

A murmur downward falls from cloudy strata
And courses over boughs and foliage grey.
It is the speech of those immortal creatures
Whose only life is boxed in ballad rhyme,
Who have not known opacities of matter,
        But born into a song
        Existence there prolong
Until disruption break the flow of mortal time.

I see them luminous within the branches.
Oh, sorrowful their eyes beyond all words!
Pale daughters of the cot and woodland castle,
And she that reigned beyond the flight of birds,
Lovers that bear the signature of sorrow—
The drowned in dowie Yarrow, and Helen, slain—
And men that from explosive surge of nature
        Bloodied the wrathful brand—
        Edward that fled the land,
And the knight whose whitened bones echoed the corbie's mane.

And one there comes that's garlanded in blossom
And sways like lilies under shade of reeds,
And seems to hold the essence of their sorrow
And for their saining and atonement pleads.
It is the child whose dying Death affrighted,
And made old horror veil his baleful eye—
The child that on the bloody spear of Gordon
        Fell from the flaming tower,
        Her ruined April hour
Wrecked on her mother's doomed and agonising cry.

Created in an artery's pulsation
From present mood and memory of place,
These shades of being vivid and dynamic
Fashion a mould of calm upon my face.

Their mass absorbs my singular existence
And unifies the heritage of pain,
And though they flash and fade in but one instant,
    Within my mind secure
    Their vision will endure
Impressed on images of Tinto under veils of rain.

STONES

The stones in Jordan's stream
Perceived the dove descend
In its lily of light;
That glory entered
Their interminable dream.

The stones in Edom's wilderness
Observed the fiend
Take five of their number
And build a cairn thereof,
And beckoning to Jesus
He pointed to the stones and said:
'Make bread.'
But because of his great love
For the uniqueness of created things,
The confraternity in disparity
Of plant and rock, of flesh and wings,
Jesus would not translate the stones
Out of their immobile immortality
Into that dynasty of death,
Decaying bread;
And the stones were gratified
And shone underneath his tread.

The stones upon Golgotha's hill
Took the shadow of the Cross
Upon them like the scorch of ice;

And they felt the flick of dice
And Jesus' blood mingling with His mother's tears;
And these made indelible stains,
And some of them were taken up
And with curses thrown
At that rejected Throne,
And others felt the clamorous butts of Roman spears:
And the pity, horror, and love within them pent
Welled out and shook the earth.
And the veil was rent.

The great stones of the tomb
Enfolded Jesus' body
In silence and deep gloom.
They had Him to themselves alone,
That shard of Him, sinew and bone,
Transient dust on their immortality.
And now their inanimate heart
Yearned over that shrouded form:
And while three midnights passed
They made of that tomb
A womb:
The fragile bones renewed their strength,
The flesh trembled and moved,
The glory of the dove
Re-descended from above,
And with the break of day
The door was rolled away:
The function of the stones was done:
His second birth
Achieved on earth,
Jesus walked into the sun.

NATIVE ELEMENT

A cloud walking.
                    Thus a child had said
Watching the landward progress of a swan
Emerge in drip of silver from a pond,
Questing sweet roots and grasses succulent.

And as the bird advanced with serpent head
Elatedly he seemed to entertain
The self-same thought. But almost instantly
His cumber'd carriage and his weighted bones
Dissuaded him. A thousand ages bent
Their arc on him. The brontosaurus moved
In his deliberate web-footed gait:
He was the essence of ungainliness.

Returned now. Oxen-wise in reeds he knelt,
And thrusting forth the snowdrift of his breast
Upon the silver water fell to rest,
At one again with his own element.

Now all the lissomness of wind and wave
Was gathered in his beauty and his pride,
No hint of any clumsiness was there,
But all was poised to perfect functioning.
He paused, and shook the glory of each wing,
And then in stillness glided on, within
His sky the sole majestic Jupiter.

GUDE SAKES

Gude sakes! It were a glammer'd thing,
    Seein' a star frae wast gang east,
    Or at the beddin' o' the sun
    Seein' the licht o' day increased!

And yet, lass, at an antrin time
We've seen the god wi' flichtert hair
Mak sic a love-lowe in the nicht,
We thocht eternal noon stood there!

WILLIAM SOUTAR

THE GOWK

Half doun the hill where fa's the linn,
 Far frae the flaught of fowk,
I saw upon a lanely whin,
 A lanely singin' gowk!
  Cuckoo, cuckoo;
Behind my back
The howie hill stuid up and spak,
  Cuckoo, cuckoo.

There was nae soun', the loupin' linn
 Was frostit in its fa';
Nae bird was on the lanely whin
 Sae white with fleurs o' snaw.
  Cuckoo, cuckoo;
I stuid stane still
And gently spak the howie hill
  Cuckoo, cuckoo.

BALLAD

O! shairly ye hae seen my love
Doun whaur the waters wind:
He walks like ane wha fears nae man
And yet his e'en are kind.

O! shairly ye hae seen my love
At the turnin' o' the tide;
For then he gethers in the nets
Doun by the waterside.

O! lassie I hae seen your love
At the turnin' o' the tide;
And he was wi' the fisher-folk
Doun by the waterside.

The fisher-folk were at their trade
No far from Walnut Grove;
They gether'd in their dreepin' nets
And found your ain true love.

THE TRYST

O luely, luely, cam she in
And luely she lay doun:
I kent her be her caller lips
And her breists sae sma' and roun'.

A' thru the nicht we spak nae word
Nor sinder'd bane frae bane:
A' thru the nicht I heard her hert
Gang soundin' wi' my ain.

It was about the waukrife hour
When cocks begin to craw
That she smool'd saftly thru the mirk
Afore the day wud daw.

Sae luely, luely, cam she in
Sae luely was she gaen;
And wi' her a' my simmer days
Like they had never been.

THE THOCHT

Young Janie was a strappin' lass
    Wha deed in jizzen-bed,
And monie a thocht her lover thocht
    Lang eftir she was dead;

But aye, wi' a' he brocht to mind
    O' misery and wrang,
There was a gledness gathered in
    Like the owrecome o' a sang:

And, gin the deid are naethingness
    Or they be minded on,
As hinny to a hungry ghaist
    Maun be a thocht like yon.

WAIT FOR THE HOUR

(to a poet)

When day follows inarticulate day;
When the mind would speak
But the heart has nought to say—
Wait for the hour.
Wait for the hour
Nor fret against the sense
Which is more old, more wise than intelligence.
O thrust not forth your word
Like a driven bird
Which braves its fledgeling breast to the blasts of the air;
Which strains an awkward wing
To meet the spring
While yet the fields are broken and the boughs are bare.
Wait for the hour;
As, hoarded within the bud,
The leaves must wait if they would bear a flower:

As wait earth's waters till their strength can flood
Under the moon.
Wait for the hour:
It is not late nor soon,
But this your power—
To curb the fretful brain and trust the blood.

MIRACLE

Summer
Is on the hill;
But in the moveless air
The fountain of the hawthorn hangs
With frost.

THE PERMANENCE OF THE YOUNG MEN

No man outlives the grief of war
Though he outlive its wreck:
Upon the memory a scar
Through all his years will ache.

Hopes will revive when horrors cease;
And dreaming dread be stilled;
But there shall dwell within his peace
A sadness unannulled.

Upon his world shall hang a sign
Which summer cannot hide:
The permanence of the young men
Who are not by his side.

WILLIAM MONTGOMERIE

SONNET AFTER SILENCE

Were moon a month about this earth my nights
Were world a year around the sun my days
Of calendars
        of diaries
                seven flights
Of pigeons round the Kremlin
                    crimson rays
Seven of a star
              eight from the Baltic out
Is now a needle quivering on a chart
Dog tail of earth
              the circus roundabout
The shilling gyroscope that's come apart
Tongues swallow their serpent tails and are
Nothing
           windowed silence looks at the sky
In pencilled cobwebs hung from star to star
The spiders of the constellations die

Within these sockets where the eyes were dull
I twist a feather duster in a skull.

ELEGY

(for William Soutar)

A narrowing of knowledge to one window to a door
Swinging inward on a man in a windless room
On a man inwardly singing
                on a singing child
Alone and never alone a lonely child

Singing
in a mirror dancing to a dancing child
Memory sang and words in a mimic dance
Old words were young and a child sang.

A narrowing of knowledge to one room to a doorway
To a door in a wall swinging bringing him friends
A narrowing of knowledge to
an arrow in bone in the marrow
An arrow
death
strung on the string of the spine.

To the live crystal in the palm and the five fingers
To the slow thirty years' pearl in the hand
Shelled in a skull in the live face of a statue
Sea-flowered on the neck of broken marble
Sunken fourteen years in that aquarium.

RUTHVEN TODD

PERSONAL HISTORY: FOR MY SON

O my heart is the unlucky heir of the ages
And my body is unwillingly the secret agent
Of my ancestors; those content with their wages
From history: the Cumberland Quaker whose gentle
Face was framed with lank hair to hide the ears
Cropped as a punishment for his steadfast faith,
The Spanish lady who had seen the pitch lake's broth
In the West Indian island, and the Fife farmers
To whom the felted barley meant a winter's want.

My face presents my history, and its sallow skin
Is parchment for the Edinburgh lawyer's deed:
To have and hold in trust, as feeofee therein
Until such date as the owner shall have need
Thereof. My brown eyes are jewels I cannot pawn,
And my long lip once curled beside an Irish bog,
My son's whorled ear was once my father's, then mine;
I am the map of a campaign, each ancestor has his flag
Marking an advance or a retreat. I am their seed.

As I write I look at the five fingers of my hand,
Each with its core of nacre bone, and rippled nails;
Turn to the palm and the traced unequal lines that end
In death—only at the tips my ancestry fails—
The dotted swirls are original and are my own:
Look at this fringed polyp which I daily use
And ask its history, ask to what grave abuse
It has been put: perhaps it curled about the stone
Of Cain. At least it has known much of evil.

And perhaps as much of good, been tender
When tenderness was needed, and been firm
On occasion, and in its past been free of gender,
Been the hand of a mother holding the warm
Impress of the child against her throbbing breast,
Been cool to the head inflamed in fever,
Sweet and direct in contact with a lover.
O in its cupped and fluted shell lies all the past,
My fingers close about the crash of history's storm.

In the tent of night I hear the voice of Calvin
Expending his hatred of the world in icy winds;
Man less than red ant beneath the towering mountain,
And God a troll more fearful than the feudal lords;

The Hugenots in me, flying Saint Bartholomew's Day,
Are in agreement with all this, and their resentful hate
Flames brighter than the candles on an altar, the grey
Afternoon is lit by Catherine wheels of terror, the street
Drinks blood, and pity is death before their swords.

The cantilever of my bones acknowledges the architect,
My father, to whom always the world was a mystery
Concealed in the humped base of a bottle, one solid fact
To set against the curled pages and the tears of history.
I am a Border keep, a croft and a solicitor's office,
A country rectory, a farm and a drawing board:
In me, as in so many, the past has stowed its miser's hoard,
Won who knows where nor with what loaded dice.
When my blood pulses it is their blood I feel hurry.

These forged me, the latest link in a fertile chain,
With ends that run so far that my short sight
Cannot follow them, nor can my weak memory claim
Acquaintance with the earliest shackle. In my height
And breadth I hold my history, and then my son
Holds my history in his small body and the history of another,
Who for me has no contact but that of flesh, his mother.
What I make now I make, indeed, from the unknown,
A blind man spinning furiously in the web of night.

IN SEPTEMBER, 1937

Coming in September, through the thin streets,
I thought back to another year I knew,
Autumn, lifting potatoes and stacking peats
On Mull, while the Atlantic's murky blue
Swung sluggishly in past Jura, and the hills
Were brown lions, crouched to meet the autumn gales.

In the hard rain and the rip of thunder,
I remember the haze coming in from the sea
And the clatter of Gaelic voices by the breakwater,
Or in the fields as the reapers took their tea;
I remembered the cast foal lying where it died,
Which we buried, one evening, above high tide:

And the three rams that smashed the fank-gate,
Running loose for five days on the moor
Before we could catch them—far too late
To prevent an early lambing the next year.
But these seemed out of place beside the chip-shop
And the cockney voices grumbling in the pub.

In September, I saw the drab newsposters
Telling of wars, in Spain and in the East,
And wished I'd stayed on Mull, their gestures
Frightened me and made me feel the unwanted guest,
The burden on the house who having taken salt
Could never be ejected, however grave his fault.

In September, we lit the fire and talked together,
Discussing the trivialities of a spent day
And what we would eat. I forgot the weather
And the dull streets and the sun on Islay,
And all my fear. I lost my carefully-kept count
Of the ticks to death, and, in September, was content.

WATCHING YOU WALK

Watching you walk slowly across a stage,
Suddenly I am become aware of all the past;
Of all the tragic maids and queens of every age,
Of Joan, whose love the flames could not arrest.

73

Of those to whom always love was the first duty,
Who saw behind the crooked world the ugly and weak,
Whose kindliness was no gesture; no condescending pity
Could rule their actions; those whom Time broke,

But whom he could not totally destroy.
Hearing the truth you give to these dead words,
Whose writer feared the life they might enjoy,
I can recall the mating orchestra of birds

Behind your voice, as lying by the lake,
You read me Owen, and I, too deeply moved,
Watched the swans for a moment, before I spoke
The trivialities, unable to tell you how I loved.

Watching your fingers curl about a painted death,
I am suddenly glad that it is April, that you are queen
Of all the sordid marches of my bruised heart,
That, loving you, the poplars never seemed to green.

Glad of my lonely walk beside the shrunken river,
Thinking of you while seeing the tufts of ash,
The chestnut candles and unreal magnolia's wax flower;
Glad that, in loving you, the whole world lives afresh.

VARIOUS ENDS

Sidney, according to report, was kindly hearted
    When stretched upon the field of death;
And, in his gentleness, ignored the blood that spurted,
    Expending the last gutter of his flickering breath.

Marlowe, whose raw temper used to rise
    Like boiling milk, went on the booze;
A quick word and his half-startled eyes
    Mirrored his guts flapping on his buckled shoes.

Swift went crazy in his lonely tower,
    Where blasphemous obscenity paid the warders,
Who brought a string of visitors every hour
    To see the wild beast, the Dean in holy orders.

And there were those coughed out their sweet soft lungs
    Upon the mountains, or the clear green sea.
Owen found half-an-ounce of lead with wings;
    And Tennyson died quietly, after tea.

Sam Johnson scissored at the surgeon's stitches
    To drain more poison from his bloated body.
And Byron may have recalled the pretty bitches,
    Nursing his fevered head in hands unsteady.

De Nerval finished swinging from a grid
    And round his neck the Queen of Sheba's garter.
Swinburne died of boredom, doing as he was bid,
    And Shelley bobbed lightly on the Mediterranean water.

Rimbaud, his leg grown blue and gross and round,
    Lay sweating for these last weeks on his truckle-bed;
He could not die—the future was unbroken ground—
    Only Paris, Verlaine and poetry were dead.

Blake had no doubts, his old fingers curled
    Around dear Kate's frail and transparent hand;
Death merely meant a changing of his world,
    A widening of experience, for him it marked no end.

TO A VERY BEAUTIFUL LADY

And when you walk the world lifts up its head,
Planets are haloed by the unembarrassed stars,
The town lies fallow at your feet, the ancient dead
Recall their loves, their queens and emperors,
Their shepherds and the quiet pastoral scene.
For less than you Troy burned and Egypt fell,
The corn was blasted while it still stood green,
And Faustus went protesting into Hell.

Be careful, sweet, adored by half the world,
Time to its darlings is not always kind,
There lie the lovelies whom the years have scored
Deeper than all the hearts which once repined.
The knife you hold could cut an empire low
Or in your own breast place the suicidal blow.

ANN SCOTT-MONCRIEFF

A NIGHT IN THE COUNTRY

Oh what a glister's to the wintry night!
Whan a' the company are gleg and bien.
In the fank o' silence made by mountains
They're birlan wi' an oorie quean.

They're birlan doon a yellow wine
Far glintier nor her hair,
And aye their sauls are gashant wi' laughter,
And aye she laughs the mair.

Oh whativer mak's the anaphrodisiac-
al wine sae sig and warm?
Tyned floors gied their deemless pooer
Wi' lees o' love for barm.

Up raves the fire more roary than the host,
It rouchles in the lum, and
Glims in gawsy glass, and luely in their e'en
Mid brash and bummand!

LINES WRITTEN IN AUTUMN, 1940

Split, heart, split, like the gowk chestnut,
Cast off the nylded spottered shell,
Those spongey barbs that you know well
Were never yet received, but
Grow interiorly from vanity.
Green, splumed-out, surface-deep,
Sad stucco growths! You yet must threep
Real agony to reach reality.
The shelter of these splaying leaves
Won't last you long
Though now they seem so strong
Streaked by the wind, a giant's neaves.
So leap, heart, leap, split and bound,
Splairge on this new autumn stoney frosted ground.
Break, heart, break—for skinkling store
Of pebble-truth within, for seed,
The brown bright bairnie's bead,
The smooth infinity of core.

GEORGE CAMPBELL HAY

BISEARTA

Chì mi ré geàrd na h-oidhche
dreòs air chrith 'na fhroidhneas thall air fàire,
ag clapail le a sgiathaibh,
a' sgapadh s ag ciaradh rionnagan na h-àird' ud.

Shaoileadh tu gu'n cluinnte,
ge cian, o 'bhuillsgein ochanaich no caoineadh
ràn corruich no gàir fuatha,
comhart chon cuthaich uaith no ulfhairt fhaolchon,
gu'n ruigeadh drannd an fhòirneirt
o'n fhùirneis òmair iomall fhéin an tsaoghail;
ach sud a' dol an leud e
ri oir an speur an tosdachd olc is aognuidh.

C'ainm an nochd a th'orra,
na sràidean bochda anns an sgeith gach uinneag
a lasraichean s a deatach,
a sradagan is sgreadail a luchd thuinidh,
is taigh air thaigh 'ga reubadh
am broinn a chéile am brùchdadh toit' a' tuiteam?
Is có an nochd tha'g atach
am Bàs a theachd gu grad 'nan cainntibh uile,
no a' spàirn measg chlach is shailthean
air bhàinidh ag gairm air cobhair, is nach cluinnear?
Có an nochd a phàigheas
sean chìs àbhaisteach na fala cumant?

Uair dearg mar lod na h-àraich,
uair bàn mar ghile thràighte an eagail éitigh,
a' dìreadh s uair a' teàrnadh,

78

a' sìneadh le sitheadh àrd s ag call a mheudachd,
a' fannachadh car aitil
s ag at mar anail dhiabhuil air dhéinead,
an t-Olc 'na chridhe s 'na chuisle,
chì mi 'na bhuillean a' sìoladh s a' leum e.
Tha'n dreòs 'na oillt air fàire,
'na fhàinne ròis is òir am bun nan speuran,
a' breugnachadh s ag àicheadh
le 'shoillse sèimhe àrsaidh àrd nan reultan.

BIZERTA

from the Gaelic of George Campbell Hay
(*Scots version by Hugh MacDiarmid*)

While I'm standin' guard the nicht I see
Awa' doon yonder on the laich skyline
A restless lowe, beatin' its wings
      and scatterin' and dimmin'
A' the starns abune wi'-in reach o' its shine.

You'd think, tho' it's hine awa', there 'ud be heard
Wailin' and lamentation pourin' oot frae't,
That roarin' and screamin', and the yowlin' o' mad dogs,
'Ud come frae that amber furnace
      a' the noises o' fear and hate,
And flood the haill lift—instead o'
      which the foul glare
Juist rises and fa's alang the horizon
      in ghastly silence there.

What are the names the nicht o' thae puir streets
Whaur ilka lozen belches flame and
      soot and the screams o' the folk
As hoose eftir hoose is rent and caves
      in in a blash o' smoke?

79

And whase are the voices cryin' on
        Daith the nicht
In sae mony different tongues to come
        quick and end their plight
Or screamin' in frenzy for help and
        no' heard, hid
Under yon muckle heaps o' burnin'
        stanes and beams,
And payin' there the auld accustomed
        tax o' common bluid?

Noo reid like a battlefield puddle, noo wan
Like the dirty pallor o' fear, shootin' up and syne
Sinkin' again, I see Evil like a hammerin'
        pulse or the spasms
O' a hert in the deidthraw aye rax up
        and dwine
The fitfu' fire, a horror on the horizon, a ring
O' rose and gowd at the fit o' the lift
        belies and denies
The ancient hie beauty and peace o'
        the starns themselves
As its foul glare crines and swells.

AN SEALGAIR AGUS AN AOIS

Cuing mo dhroma an aois a nis,
    rib mo choise, robach, liath:
fear thig eadar soills' is sùilean,
    fear thig eadar rùn is gnìomh.

Fàgaidh e am faillean crotach,
    ris gach dos 's e chuireas sgian:
is, och, b' e 'm bàrr air gach miosguinn
    tighinn eadar mi 's an sliabh.

T'hug e dhiom a' Chruach Chaorainn,
　　's an gunna caol, 's an ealchainn shuas:
bhuin e dhiom mo neart, am meàirleach,
　　dh'fhàg e mi gun làmh, gun luaths.

Na'n robh aige corp a ghlacainn,
　　's na'n tachrainn ris leis fhéin 's a' bheinn,
bhiodh saltairt ann is fraoch 'ga reubadh,
　　's fuil air feur mu'n sgaradh sinn.

THE AULD HUNTER
from the Gaelic of George Campbell Hay
(*Scots version by Hugh MacDiarmid*)

Eild comes owre me like a yoke on my craig,
A girn roon' my feet, the lourd and the chill.
Betwixt my sicht and the licht it comes,
It comes betwixt the deed and the will.

This is the thing that warps the sapling
And sets its knife to the aipple's root,
But the warst deed o' a' its spite has been
To filch the hill frae under my foot.

My narrow gun and the paths o' the cruach
Eild has stown, wha's deef and heeds nae grief;
My hand and my foot, this Blear-eyed's stown them
And a' my cheer, like a hertless thief.

But gin Eild were a man that hauns could grapple
And I could come on him secretly
Up there on the hill when naebody passes
Certes! Grass 'ud be trampled or he gat free!

'Tha iad ann an grunnd na mara,
is cha b'e sud an rogha cala—'
rug sud orm o dh'fhalbh mo mhacan,
an cuilean a bhithinn 'ga thatadh,
a dhèanadh gàire 'na mo ghlacaibh.
Thàinig an seann sgeul air a chasan.
Tha 'n speur ag ciaradh mu fheasgar,
goir aig na h-eòin air na sgeirean,
geumnaich a' chruidh a' teachd dhachaidh,
éigheach nan giullan anns a' bhaile,
's mi 'm thurraman leam fhéin mu 'n chagailt,
a' smuaineachadh air na bh' agam.
Chì mi do chòta air an tarran,
is, och, an taigh gun fhuaim, gun fhacal,
an stairsneach nach bi fuaim chas oirr',
an seòmar fàs 's an leabaidh fhalamh!
Ma's e an osna a théid fada,
cluinnear m' osnaich far na laigh thu,
'nad chadal luasganach 's an fheamainn,
's na fuathan a' sìor dhol seachad,
cruthanna aognaidh na mara.

'Éisd, a bhean, is na bi rium,
is truimide mo dhìol do bhròn;
sgàin is leagh an long fo 'r buinn,
thriall an cuimhn' an cois an deò.
Lunnainn a mharbh mi,
a mhill an t-sùil nach fhaca i;
theagamh gum b'aithne dhomh thu:
sgùr an sàl mo chuimhne nis.

Tha mi air sabhd 'sa chuan mhór;
bu mhise Domhnall an dé,
laigh do ghul orm 'na lòd,
ge b'e có thu, a bhean, éisd.'

Mo losgadh, muinntir nan Eilean,
is daor a phàigh sibh mórachd Bhreatainn.

THONDER THEY LIGG
from the Gaelic of George Campbell Hay
(*Scots version by Douglas Young*)

'Thonder they ligg on the grund o the sea,
nae the hyne whaur they wald be.'
Siccan a thing has happenit me
sin my son's been gane. When he was wee
I dannlit the bairn like a whelpikie
and he leuch i ma airms richt cantilie.
It's the auld weird nou I maun dree.

The luft grows derk, the sun gangs laigh,
atour the skerries the sea-maws skreigh,
the rowtan kye come schauchlan doun,
the laddies rant out-throu the toun;
but here I rock at the fire ma lane,
mindan o him I had that's gane.

I see your jacket on the heuk,
but the hous is lown in ilka neuk,
never a sound or a word i the room,
nae sclaffan o buits on the threshart-stane,
the bed cauld and the chalmer toom.

Gin it's the sych that traivels far
ye'll hear my sychan whaur ye are,
sleepan i the wrack, jundied aye,
wi ugsome ferlies sooman by,
the ghaistlie monsters o the sea.

'Wheesht, woman, wheesht, and deavena me.
My wae's the mair to see ye greet.
The ship brak doun under our feet,
life gaed aff, and memorie wi 't.
London slew me, weary faa 't,
connacht the een that never saw it.
Aiblins I was acquent wi you,
the saut has reingit my memorie nou.

Here I stravaig i the merchless faem,
yestreen Donald was my name.
The wecht o your wae liggs sair on me.
Woman, wheesht, whae'er ye be.'

Sair the price maun be dounpitten
by the island-fowk for the greatness o Britain.

ROBERT GARIOCH

GHAISTIES

Cauld are the ghaisties in yon kirkyaird
    an' cauld the airms
that they mell wi' the mists o' the timm
        breists o' their loves;
at the heid o' their bed cauld angels staund on guaird,
    an' marble doves.

They ken na' the fear o' Gode, as they sleep ayont sin,
        nor the terror o' man
an' there's nane but the angels tae glunch
                at their trueloves' chairms,
yet they lang for the reek o' the
                creeshy swat frae the skin,
        an' the grup o' a haun'.
But we in the warld are alowe
wi' the glawmer o' bluid-reid flame
that loups ti the bluid in your tongue's tip
                as it tingles on mine,
        an' the howe
o' the back we loo wi' oor finger-tips, an' the wame,
brent-white, wi' a flush aneath
                like cramosie wine,
hoo it curves ti meet ma ain!
        O ma sonsie frow
what though the flesh be bruckle,
                an' fiends be slee,
the joys o' the solid earth we'll pree or they dwine,
we'll lauch at daith, an' man, an' the fiend, aw three,
        afore we dee.

GEORGE BRUCE

INHERITANCE

This which I write now
Was written years ago
Before my birth
In the features of my father.

It was stamped
In the rock formations
West of my hometown.
Not I write,

But, perhaps, William Bruce,
Cooper,
Perhaps here his hand
Well articled in his trade.

Then though my words
Hit out
An ebullition from
City or flower,

There not my faith,
These the paint
Smeared upon
The inarticulate,

The salt-crusted sea-boot,
The red-eyed mackerel,
The plate shining with herring,
And many men,

Seamen and craftsmen and curers,
And behind them
The protest of hundreds of years,
The sea obstinate against the land.

KINNAIRD HEAD

I go North to cold, to home, to Kinnaird,
Fit monument for our time.

This is the outermost edge of Buchan.
Inland the sea birds range,
The tree's leaf has salt upon it,
The tree turns to the low stone wall.
And here a promontory rises towards Norway,
Irregular to the top of thin grey grass
Where the spindrift in storm lays its beads.
The water plugs in the cliff sides,
The gull cries from the clouds
This is the consummation of the plain.

O impregnable and very ancient rock,
Rejecting the violence of water,
Ignoring its accumulations and strategy,
You yield to history nothing.

THE FISHERMAN

As he comes from one of those small houses
Set within the curve of the low cliff
For a moment he pauses
Foot on step at the low lintel
Before fronting wind and sun.
He carries out from within something of the dark
Concealed by heavy curtain,
Or held within the ship under hatches.

Yet with what assurance
The compact body moves,
Head pressed to wind,
His being at an angle
As to anticipate the lurch of earth.

Who is he to contain night
And still walk stubborn
Holding the ground with light feet
And with a careless gait?

Perhaps a cataract of light floods,
Perhaps the apostolic flame.
Whatever it may be
The road takes him from us.
Now the pier is his, now the tide.

SONG FOR A HERO

There is no home for the hero.
Even when a boy he left his passions
At the pier. His eyes did not note them,
Nor the white handkerchiefs, but turned,
As the North-controlled needle turns,
To the gulls who offered no memento.

Yet with the rest he had his curios,
The master key that opened all,
The starfish sporting one more limb,
The match-box with the double back,
Shells highly convoluted like a screw,
But these made exits from his heart.

And school was taken in his stride,
His gaze averted from it all,
Though capes and bays and distances
Were glanced at, recognised
As matters of potential interest.
Astronomy he was not taught.

Darkness ingathers the ship. The foam
Of many seas arches upon her bows.
The cargoes, corn for metal,
Make their change. And he takes stock,
Sees to delivery, hears the engine run,
And stands observant at the winch.

There is no home for a hero.
His head—like a head in profile,
The minted head on a coin—
Occupies the windy spaces
And holds predestined courses.

DOUGLAS YOUNG

SABBATH I THE MEARNS

The geans are fleuran whyte i the green Howe o the Mearns;
wastlan winds are blawan owre the Mownth's cauld glacks,
whaur the whaups wheep round their nesties among the fog and
      ferns;
and the ferm-touns stand gray and lown, ilk wi its yalla stacks.
The kirk is skailan, and the fowk in Sabbath stand o blacks
are doucely haudan hame til their denners wi the bairns,
the young anes daffan and auld neebours haean cracks.

Thon's bien and canty livan for auld-farrant fermer-fowk
wha wark their lives out on the land, the bonnie Laigh o Mearns.
They pleu and harra, saw and reap, clatt neeps and tattie-howk,
and dinna muckle fash theirsels wi ither fowk's concerns.
There's whiles a chyld that's unco wild, but sune the wildest
      learns
gin ye're nae a mensefu fermer-chiel ye's be naething but a gowk,
and the auld weys are siccar, auld and siccar like the sterns.

They werena aye like thon, this auld Albannach race,
whas stanes stand heich upo' the Mownth whaur the wild whaup
   caas.

Focht for libertie wi Wallace, luikit tyrants i the face,
stuid a siege wi leal Ogilvie for Scotland's king and laws,[1]
i the Whigs' Vaut o Dunnottar testified for Freedom's cause.
Is there onie Hope to equal the Memories o this place?
The last Yerl Marischal 's deid, faan doun his castle waas.

FOR A WIFE IN JIZZEN

Lassie, can ye say
    whaur ye ha been,
whaur ye ha come frae,
    whatna ferlies seen?

Eftir the bluid and swyte,
    the warsslan o yestreen,
ye ligg forfochten, whyte,
    prouder nor any queen.

Albeid ye hardly see me
    I read it in your een,
sae saft blue and dreamy,
    mindan whaur ye've been.

Anerly wives ken
    the ruits o joy and tene,
    the march o daith and birth,
        the tryst o luve and strife
    i the howdumbdeidsunsheen,
    fire, air, water, yirth
        mellan to mak new life,
    lauchan and greetan, feiman and serene.

Dern frae aa men
    the ferlies ye ha seen.

[1] Sir George Ogilvie of Barras held Dunnottar Castle, with Charles II's
regalia inside, against the Cromwellian General Monk.

ARDLOGIE, CHRISTMAS EVE, 1939

The mild midwinter evening ebbs, leaving
wreckage of gold and purple on the hill.
The full round moon sails up from eastward, cleaving
dim veils of star-split cloud, tenuous and still.

Winter has jewels yet, leaf, flower, and berry,
berberis, holly, crab, and many more;
wych-hazels' golden straps, a starry cherry,
primroses, heaths, a purple hellebore.

There's a viburnum by the porch, some vagrant
botanist found in Western Yunnan.
It's flowering now, exquisitely fragrant,
waxy white umbels, scent of marzipan.

Moon-white the naked beeches tower, wreathing
lichened limbs above the laurel glooms;
beyond the lawn a ground-air faintly breathing
stirs the white torches of the pampas plumes.

About me as I walk an odour lingers
of cypress logs I sawed; the pungent scent
clings in my tweeds, and when I raise my fingers
I get the resinous smell, and am content.

Cock-pheasants from the neighbouring pinewood chortle,
a blackbird whistles from the red-twigged lime.
There's enough pleasure here for any mortal
with eyes, ears, nose, this mild midwinter-time.

FOR THE OLD HIGHLANDS

That old lonely lovely way of living
in Highland places,—twenty years a-growing,
twenty years flowering, twenty years declining—
father to son, mother to daughter giving
ripe tradition; peaceful bounty flowing;
one harmony all tones of life combining—
old, wise ways, passed like the dust blowing.

That harmony of folk and land is shattered,—
the yearly rhythm of things, the social graces,
peat-fire and music, candle-light and kindness.
Now they are gone it seems they never mattered,
much, to the world, those proud and violent races,
clansmen and chiefs whose passioned greed and blindness
made desolate these lovely lonely places.

FIFE EQUINOX

Ae day and ae nicht a yowden-druft
fae the cauld nor-aist has whusslit and pufft
and blawn the craws about the luft,
blatteran sairlie;
it reeshlit the wuids and gart them shuft
like a breer o barley.

The cypress-busses are aa blawn cruikit,
the greens are as clorty as onie doocot;
the wind-faan epples 'll hae to be cuikit
afore they get waur.
The plooms are aa wersh, they're that sair droukit
and clortit wi glaur.

LAST LAUCH

The Minister said it wald dee,
    the cypress buss I plantit.
But the buss grew til a tree,
    naething dauntit.

It's growan, stark and heich,
    derk and straucht and sinister,
kirkyairdie-like and dreich.
    But whaur's the Minister?

J. F. HENDRY

INVERBEG

Sliced with shade and scarred with snow
A mountain breaks like Mosaic rock
And through the lilt of mist there flow
Restless rivers of pebble, pocked
And speckled, where moss and the centuries grow.

Tree, married to cloud as stem is to feather,
Branches and straddles the convex of sky.
Death is aflame in the bracken where heather
Rears semaphore smoke into high
Blue messenger fire through soundless weather.

Below, like bees, the ivies swarm,
Cast in leaping veins, their trunk, a crippled
Animal of thighs pounced from loch-water, storms
The slated shores of the past into ripples
Interpreting man's fretted cuneiform.

93

KRANJSKA GORA, SLOVENIA

1

This valley, like a cup, is filled with silence
Whose deep draught drunk makes a moment of eternity.
Its mists are chaos we bring up from the city
Yet dawn is distilled through their latent violence.

I ask the flowers and mountains what they mean
And they stand aghast, and cannot answer.
No thoughts encumber children, or a dancer.
Love needs no language to act as a screen.

2

What mad hand smashes the cup and fills these hills
With incoherent memory trailing bloodstains of pity?
What beast from earth's centre growling over eternity
Shook the valley with iron tears and silenced the watermills?

You mountains did what you could to warn the plain.
This coral spire rallied the peasants to their last fight
Like a sabre. Its bell wove still waves before their sight
And all the stones of the river stood up beside the slain.

3

Stol, melodious, whispers through the shouting distance
'How shall I control the colours of my rage
Punched into me by fists of volcanic violence?
Lost in their depths, O German, you are drowned to any age.'

'Would you hang the song winding over the meadow? Then blind
Mad children slay the trees! Strip the forest of its green!
Since you fight to win the world for black night, bind
Back in earth, stone, pine and man! Kill all! All are Slovene!'

4

Grown in this oceanic tear becalming ships
Your still whirlwind expands in summer air,
Bounteous as space, ethereal as fire where
Poppies blow again across the corn's lips.

Dawn wakes cold fountains of overflowing sun, as under
Cisterns of sleep I see how at last You come,
Starred in Your eyes the thunderbolts of freedom,
To load our darkness with light and morning wonder.

5

Lightness You hold. The silver trumpet of the moon in the eyes
Of flower and girl veils love in a bridal petal.
I cannot help remembering how the wealth of all these skies,
Mountainous in women and in men, was hammered true as metal.

Brightness You hold. The confetti air in Your hand
Stands intently assembled in star-cities and sunflowers.
I cannot help looking at Europe through these hours.
I cannot help looking with hope at this still land.

PORTRAIT OF DAVID

Out of a lightning void who clutched blue rivers
Spins a shell-flower head on sea-screened floors.
An echo coils an ear in Fingal's Cave
Along whose flickering shores he plucked his eyes
And hirples lighthouse space down pebbled chin.

His frowning knuckles doubling are the rainbow
Clenching fists of cloudy Scottish thunder.
Ribs, once wrecked ships sunk on a broken beach,
Now swell a chest of treasure in screw sand, or
Blast a southron air with Highland spleen.

Sabre-toothed, the tiger Hebrides thrust
And parry sea. That sleeping lipline pins
On space awakened purpose, is a mastodon.
A gnarled kneecap, or an elm down a glen,
Forge spring-knots for the kilted saunterers.

Out of the dark-green jar who grasped light arching,
Hoards electric sun in branching arms.
The mottled trunk-one, wrenched from silver birch,
Remembers brindling Cluny in a Braemar storm,
Fire-talk, venison, we happy winterers.

FOR LAUREO DE BOSEIS

The clouds you tore up into paper and printed in clean hail
and the white snow you suddenly showered over Rome
hid confetti for many happy marriages.
It was the minting of the new lira
from the wake of ships in the Mediterranean
and the dance of the washing in the back streets of Trieste.

In a handsturn like a conjuror
you made a banknote into a carnival hat
no wonder they were all afraid of you
your boundless happiness that could only stretch its legs in the
    heavens
was a menace to the State of Misery
you threatened their hard-won poverty.

You did not share the distrust they entered in columns of figures
    in ledgers
your elation commanded no confidence
wretchedness at least is real
and they felt safer in hell than in your mad heaven
the corn on their soles said it was a mirage
they wanted no tongue speaking through the whips.

96

How can one blame their terror of your terrible heights?
It made them giddy, they had dreams of falling,
till even your friends said you were romantic
because the light in your voice was a light
and not a reflection among the rocks.

Hovering like a kestrel or an eagle
settling on the waters without being swept away by the waters
you matched the full course of the flood of human ravage
plunging its way to drown in the Adriatic
all the houses and the clothes-lines and the pigeons and apples
    and shawls of the old women
all the bayonets and bowls and frogs and the sticks of the blind.

The junk and the paraphernalia of five hundred years of melo-
    drama
wrecked in the towsled pawnshop of the heart
and you tied up the bandages and the ice-cream and the powder-
    puffs again
with the caps of chefs and convolvulus
in the embers of your glory
and the streamers of your clouds.

TIR-NAN-OG

A man is born, a man dies,
And in between are miseries.

In between he is alive
But cannot be allowed to live

Since, body's hunger never fed,
The mind is never satisfied

And hands and feet and head and eyes
Are hourly humbled to the knees.

A man dies, a man is born,
And in between a burden borne.

In between, by force of love,
A grief in life is made alive

Whose mind is more than satisfied
And body's hunger always fed,

Whose hands rise up from feet and knees,
Encircle head and rub the eyes.

THE SHIP

Here is a ship you made
Out of my breast and sides
As I lay dead in the yards
Under the hammers.

Here is the hull you built
Out of a heart of salt,
Sky-rent, the prey of birds
Strung on the longshore.

Here is her rigging bound
Nerve, sinew, ice and wind
Blowing through the night
The starred dew of beads.

Here her ribs of silver
Once steerless in a culvert
Climb the laddered centuries
To hide a cloud in a frame.

THE CONSTANT NORTH

(For Dee)

Encompass me, my lover,
With your eyes' wide calm.
Though noonday shadows are assembling doom,
The sun remains when I remember them;
And death, if it should come,
Must fall like quiet snow from such clear skies.

Minutes we snatched from the unkind winds
Are grown into daffodils by the sea's
Edge, mocking its green miseries;
Yet I seek you hourly still, over
A new Atlantis loneliness, blind
As a restless needle held by the constant north
      we always have in mind.

SORLEY MACLEAN

DAIN DO EIMHIR LIV.

Bu tu camhanaich air a' Chuilthionn
's latha suilbhir air a' Chlàraich,
grian air a h-uilinn anns an òr-shruth
agus ròs geal bristeadh fàire.

Lainnir sheòl air linne ghrianaich,
gorm a' chuain is iarmailt àr-bhuidh,
an òg-mhaduinn 'na do chuailean
's 'na do ghruaidhean soilleir àlainn.

99

Mo leug camhanaich is oidhche
t' aodann 's do choibhneas gràdhach,
ged tha bior glas an dòlais
troimh chliabh m' òg-mhaidne sàthte.

YE WERE THE DAWN

from the Gaelic of Sorley Maclean
(*Scots version by Douglas Young*)

Ye were the dawn on the hills o the Cuillin,
the bousum day on the Clarach arisan,
the sun on his elbucks i the gowden flume,
the whyte rose-fleur that braks the horizon.

Gesserant sails on a skinklan frith,
gowd-yalla lyft and blue o the sea . . .
the fresh mornan in your heid o hair
and your clear face wi its bonnie blee.

Gowdie, my gowdie o dawn and the derk
your loesome gentrice, your brou sae rare . . .
albeid wi the dullyart stang o dule
the breist o youth 's been thirlit sair.

CALBHARAIGH

Cha n-eil mo shùil air Calbharaigh
no air Bethlehem an àigh
ach air cùil ghrod an Glaschu
far bheil an lobhadh fàis
agus air seòmar an Dun-éideann,
seòmar bochdainn 's cràidh
far am bheil an naoidhean creuchdach
ri aonagraich gu 'bhàs.

MY EEN ARE NAE ON CALVARY

from the Gaelic of Sorley Maclean
(*Scots version by Douglas Young*)

My een are nae on Calvary
or the Bethlehem they praise,
but on shitten back-lands in Glesga toun
whaur growan life decays,
and a stairheid room in an Embro land,
a chalmer o puirtith and skaith,
whaur monie a shilpet bairnikie
gaes smoorit doun til daith.

BAN-GHAIDHEAL

Am faca Tu i, Iudhaich mhóir,
ri an abrar Aon Mhac Dhé?
Am fac' thu a coltas air Do thriall
ri strì an fhìon-lios chéin?

An cuallach mheasan air a druim,
fallus searbh air mala is gruaidh;
's a' mhios chreadha trom air cùl
a cinn chrùibte, bhochd, thruaigh.

Chan-fhaca Tu i, Mhic an t-saoir,
ri an abrar Rìgh na Glòir,
am measg nan cladach carrach, siar,
fo fhallus cliabh a lòin.

An t-earrach so agus so chaidh
's gach fichead earrach bho an tùs
tharruing ise an fheamainn fhuar
chum biadh a cloinn is duais an tùir.

101

Is gach fichead foghar tha air triall
chaill i samhradh buidh nam blàth;
is threabh an dubh chosnadh an clais
tarsuinn mìnead ghil a clàr.

Agus labhair T' eaglais chaomh
mu staid chaillte a h-anama thruaigh;
agus leag an cosnadh dian
a corp gu sàmchair dhuibh an uaigh.

Is thriall a tìm mar shnighe dubh
a' drùdhadh tughaidh fàrdaich bochd;
mheal ise an dubh chosnadh cruaidh;
is glas a cadal suain an nochd.

HIELANT WOMAN

from the Gaelic of Sorley Maclean
(*Scots version by Douglas Young*)

Hae ye seen her, ye unco Jew,
ye that they caa Ae Son o God?
Thon trauchlit woman i the far vine-yaird,
saw ye the likes o her on your road?

A creelfu o corn upo her spaul,
swyte on her brou, saut swyte on her cheek,
a yirthen pat on the tap o her heid,
her laigh bouit heid, dwaiblie and sick.

Ye haena seen her, ye son o the vricht,
wi 'King o Glory' fowk roose ye weel,
on the staney westland machars thonder
swytan under her wechtit creel.

This spring o the year is by and gane
and twenty springs afore it spent,
sin she's hikeit creels o cauld wrack
for her bairns' meat and the laird's rent.

102

Twenty hairsts hae dwineit awa,
she's tint her simmer's gowden grace,
while the sair trauchle o the black wark
pleud its rigg on her clear face.

Her puir saul is eternallie tint,
as threeps aye your kindly Kirk;
and endless wark has brocht her corp
to the graff's peace, lown and derk.

Her time gaed by like black sleek
through an auld thaikit hous-rig seepan;
she bruikit aye sair black wark,
and gray the nicht is her lang sleepan.

AN TROM-LAIGHE

Oidhche de 'n dà bhliadhna
'N uair shaoil mi gun do chreuchdadh
Mo luaidh le giamh cho miosa
'S a bh' air mnaoi bho linn Eubha,
Bha sinn comhla am bruadar
Ri taobh a' bhalla chloiche
Tha eadar cluich ghart ghillean
Is nighean mo cheud sgoile,
Bha i eadar mo lamhan
'S mo bheul a' dol g'a bilibh
'N uair straon an ceann oillteil
Bho chul a' bhalla 'n clisgeadh,
Is rinn na cràgan ciara
Fada bréine mo sgornan
A ghlacadh an greim obann
'S lean briathran an eu-dochais:
"Tha thu ghloic air dheireadh."

THE WIDDREME

from the Gaelic of Sorley Maclean

(*Scots version by Sydney Smith*)

Ae nicht o thae twa year
Whan I thocht ma luve
Was strak wi a skaith as dure
As wumman's had sen Eve,
We were thegither in a dwaum
By the stane dyke that stauns
Atween the loons' and lassies' yairds
O ma first schuil.
          Ma airms
Were round her an ma lips
Seekan her mou
Whan the laithlie gorgon's heid stuid up
On a sudden frae hint the waa,
An the lang mirk ugsome fingers graipt
Ma craig wi a sidden grup—
An than the words o weirdless dule:
'Owre blate, ye fuil!'

SYDNEY GOODSIR SMITH

LOCH LEVEN

Tell me was a glorie ever seen
As the morn I left ma lass
'Fore licht i the toun o snaw
And saw the daw
O' burnan crammassie
Turn the gray ice
O' Mary's Loch Leven
Tae sheenan bress—

An kent the glorie and the gleen
Was but the waukenan o her een?

LARGO

Ae boat anerlie nou
Fishes frae this shore,
Ae black drifter lane
Riggs the crammassie daw—
Aince was a fleet, and nou
Ae boat alane gaes out.

War ir peace, the trawlers win
An the youth turns awa
Bricht wi baubles nou
An thirled tae factory ir store;
Their faithers fished their ain,
Unmaistered; ane remains.

And never the clock rins back,
The free days are owre;
The warld shrinks, we luik
Mair t'oor maisters ilka hour—
Whan yon lane boat I see
Daith and rebellion blinn ma ee.

MA MOUJIK LASS

Ma hert is lowpan owre the trees
    An fleean wi the wund—
Ma lips 're weet wi barley bree,
    Ma hurdies hug the grund.

The lass I loo has turned awa,
    Tae me yon hert's a stane—
But fain I'd hae her fause an aa
    Than bidan here alane.

Some airt the linties maun be singan,
    Here the wuids are toom,
And aye the rain is dingan, dingan,
    Dingan on the toun.

O fain I'd loo ma moujik lass,
    O fain I'd haud her breist—
I've nocht tae haud but a whisky glass,
    A gey wanchancy feast.

Och dreich's the exile here I sing,
    The lyft is mirk aroun,
And aye I hear the raindraps ding,
    Aye dingan on the toun.

SAHARA

(Efter hearan Sibelius' Fift Symphonie)

I

Inexorable on ye stride,
Fate, lik' a desart wund;
Agin yir vast unpassioned pride
I pit ma saul an haund,
As the wild Bedouin
Tykes gowl at the muin.

II

March, ye luveless Cailleach, blaw
Til the dumbest, mirkest end,
An whan the yerth's a blastit skau
As toom Sahara brunt an blinnd
Thare, daft and damned wi raivan ee,
Adam, greinan tae be free.

SPLEEN

Steir bogle, squat bogle
Bogle o sweirness an stuperie;
Wersh bogle, wae bogle,
Bogle o drumlie apathie;
Thir twa haud this fule in duress——
Malancolie, Idleness.

In duress vile ye muckil fule,
Cock o yir midden o sloth an stour,
Geck o the yill an a restless saul
I dwaum lik a convict, dowf an dour
As the runt o a riven aik
Whaur ghouls can set or their hurdies ache.

The westlins sun, reid owre The Gowf,
Fluids the Links wi glaumerie,
I set wi ma bogles dour an dowf,
Idleness an Malancolie;
Lik a braw new penny Sol dwines doun
Fou lik ma hert—but the saul toom.

WHAN THE HERT IS LAICH

Lamb, whan the hert is laich,
Lourd wi the haill warld's wecht,
A boulder's whare the hert shud be,
A muckle stane that burdens ye.

Ye sit lik' a cairn o stane yersel,
The burds' blye sangs ye hear wi laith,
The saikless burn rins doun tae hell,
The aince-luved trees a choir o daith.

An whitna cause ye mayna tell
Nor casting reasoun bring release,
Ye sit lik' a stane an watch the hills
That mock yir thrawan wi their peace.

ADAM DRINAN

SUCCESSFUL SCOT

Gold pins and pearls of Columbia,
            how gross they grow by your drive,
studding an English summer
            with the back-end of your life,
                        beknighted and pompous Scot!

By adding figure to figure
            you have developed never,
you have just grown bigger and bigger
            like this wee wort from the heather;
                        and size is all you have got.

Your mind set towards London,
            your belly pushing to success,
from the very day that you won
            the Bursary of the West,
                        have flagged and faltered not.

Not much has your face altered!
            The man has the mouth of the child.
The Position you planted and watered
            expands from the lad's desires
                        as if bound in a pot.

And would you return (for the fishing)
        to your island of humbler hours,
there in your tailored wishes
        you would trample your youth in this flower
            that you have forgotten:

Or spending a stay-at-home summer,
        you will never know what they suffer,
these bloated flowers of Columbia;
        you will own the youth of others,
            and never know what.

from
THE MEN ON THE ROCKS

Our pastures are bitten and bare
our wool is blown to the winds
our mouths are stopped and dumb
our oatfields weak and thin.
Nobody fishes the loch
nobody stalks the deer.
Let us go down to the sea.
The friendly sea likes to be visited.

Our fathers sleep in the cemetery
their boats, cracked, by their side.
The sea turns round in his sleep
pleasurecraft nod on the tide.
Sea ducks slumber on waves
sea eagles have flown away.
Let us put out to sea.
The fat sea likes to be visited.

Fat sea, what's on your shelf?
all the grey night we wrestled.
To muscle, to skill, to petrol,
Hook oo rin yo! . . . one herring!
and of that only the head.
Dogfishes had the rest,
A parting gift from the sea.
The merry waves like to be visited.

Merry sea, what have you sent us?
A rusty English trawler?
The crew put into the hotel
the engineer overhauls her.
Gulls snatch offal to leeward.
We on the jetty await
gifts of the cod we can't afford . . .
The free sea likes to be visited.

Free were our fathers' boats
whose guts were strown on the shore.
Steam ships were bought by the rich
cheap from the last war.
They tear our nets to pieces
and the sea gives them our fishes.
Even he favours the rich.
The false sea likes to be visited.

from
THE GHOSTS OF THE STRATH

Long blue shadow of salmon lying,
    shot shell of leaping silver,
using the lull and the flies
    to practise for the rough river,
stay down on the salt sea stones,
    learn there, you yet-free fishes.

Your sweet hope to come home
    was once on the hillside fishers.

Salmon may leap falls;
    we deeps of the linn may master:
but weeds grow up our walls,
    hearts whip in airy water.
Up in the rich meads
    such the rich men's power is,
Only wrens are safe in streams
    and sheep in houses.

The great power, had its magic!
    with strong spells of paper
money and law raised lairds;
    burnt crops bewitched labour.
No cunning of fish-lore
    will conjure our safe return;
but the same black arts be ours—
    from the need to burn, to the burning.

MEASURES

Three measures of breadth I take
that the heart, the hand, and the foot make:
    the candid inches between the eyes of confidence,
    the width of a gull's back in the hand that shot it,
    and the stretch of a water that cannot be walked upon.

And three measures of slenderness I put to these,
in which the eye, the ear, and the mind meet:
    the slimness of a boy's ankle while he is alive to dance,
    the whisper that draws a hill across a strath,
    and that which separates self-respect from self-regard.

LOVE SONG

Soft as the wind your hair,
gull-gleaming your breasts.
I hoard no treasures there.
I do not grope for rest.
I seek you as my home,
that all your sensitive life
may fuse into my own,
and the world match with my wife.

I carry you out of this
to no enchanted isle.
Blood is tart in your kiss,
and no dream in your smile.
Bitter, bitter the hours
and coasts of our patrol.
Foggy this Minch of ours.
But I sail with your soul.

I come to you in the flame
of a burst and broken land.
There is acid in my brain
and withering in my hand.
Your touch will plot us wise,
your quiet keep it true;
and joy be the starlight
to what we have to do.

G. S. FRASER

MEDITATION OF A PATRIOT

The posters show my country blonde and green,
Like some sweet siren, but the travellers know
How dull the shale sky is, the airs how keen,
And how our boorish manners freeze like snow.
Romantic Scotland was an emigrant,
Half-blooded, and escaped from sullen weather.
Here, we toss off a dram to drown a cough
And whisky has the trade-mark of the heather.
My heart yearns southwards as the shadows slant,
I wish I were an exile and I rave:
        With Byron and with Lermontov
        Romantic Scotland's in the grave.

In Glasgow, that damned sprawling evil town,
I interview a vulgar editor,
Who, brawny, self-made, looks me up and down
And seems to wonder what my sort is for.
Do I write verse? Ah, man, but that is bad . . .
And, too polite, I fawn upon this tough,
But when I leave him, O my heart is sad.
He sings alone who in this province sings.
I kick a lamp-post, and in drink I rave:
        With Byron and with Lermontov
        Romantic Scotland's in the grave.

In the far islands to the north and west
Mackenzie and MacDiarmid have their peace.
St. Andrews soothes that critic at her breast
Whose polished verse ne'er gave his soul release.
I have no islands and no ancient stone,
Only the sugary granite glittering crisp
Pleases the eye, but turns affection off,
Hard rhetoric, that never learned to lisp.

This town has beauty, but I walk alone
And to the flat and sallow sands I rave:
  With Byron and with Lermontov
  Romantic Scotland's in the grave.

TO HUGH MACDIARMID

Since mine was never the heroic gesture,
  Trained to slick city from my childhood's days,
Only a rambling garden's artful leisure
  Giving my mind its privacy and ease.

Since Poverty for me has never sharpened
  Her single tooth, and since Adversity
So far has failed to jab me with her hair-pin,
  I marvel who my Scottish Muse can be.

I am Convention's child, the cub reporter,
  The sleek, the smooth, conservatively poised:
Abandoned long ago by Beauty's daughter;
  Tamed like a broncho, and commercialised!

Perhaps I have a heart that feels ... I wonder!
  At least I can salute your courage high,
Your thought that burns language to a cinder,
  Your anger, and your angry poet's joy.

O warrior, with the world and wind against you,
  Old sea-bird, in your bleak and rocky coign,
Only my fears can follow where you fly to ...
  Beneath these rocks, how many souls lie slain!

Your journey has not been the private journey
  Through a mad loveliness, of Hölderlin.
Against the windmills, sir, you chose to tourney.
  And yet, by marvellous chance, you hold your own.

O true bright sword! Perhaps, like Mithridates,
  Before the night has fallen, you may say:
'Now I am satisfied: at least, my hate is:
  Now let me die: I saw the English flee.'

Facing boys' faces, whom your world of thunder
  Is massing clouds for, whom the violet forks
Seek out from heaven . . . simulating candour
  I face both ways! A secret question carks.

Because my love was never for the common
  But only for the rare, the singular air,
Or the undifferenced and naked human,
  Your Keltic mythos shudders me with fear.

What a race has is always crude and common,
  And not the human or the personal:
I would take sword up only for the human,
  Not to revive the broken ghosts of Gael.

LEAN STREET

Here, where the baby paddles in the gutter,
  Here, in the slaty greyness and the gas,
Here where the women wear dark shawls and mutter
  A hasty word as other women pass,

Telling the secret, telling, clucking and tutting,
  Sighing, or saying that it served her right,
The bitch!—the words and weather both are cutting
  In Causewayend, on this November night.

At pavement's end and in the slaty weather
  I stare with glazing eyes at meagre stone,
Rain and the gas are sputtering together
  A dreary tune! O leave my heart alone,

115

O leave my heart alone, I tell my sorrows,
  For I will soothe you in a softer bed
And I will numb your grief with fat to-morrows
  Who break your milk teeth on this stony bread!

They do not hear. Thought stings me like an adder,
  A doorway's sagging plumb-line squints at me,
The fat sky gurgles like a swollen bladder
  With the foul rain that rains on poverty.

HOME TOWN ELEGY
(For Aberdeen in Spring)

Glitter of mica at the windy corners,
Tar in the nostrils, under blue lamps budding
Like bubbles of glass and blue buds of a tree,
Night-shining shopfronts, or the sleek sun flooding
The broad abundant dying sprawl of the Dee:
For these and for their like my thoughts are mourners
That yet shall stand, though I come home no more,
Gas-works, white ballroom, and the red brick baths
And salmon nets along a mile of shore,
Or beyond the municipal golf-course, the moorland paths
And the country lying quiet and full of farms.
This is the shape of a land that outlasts a strategy
And is not to be taken with rhetoric or arms.
Or my own room, with a dozen books on the bed
(Too late, still musing what I mused, I lie
And read too lovingly what I have read),
Brantome, Spinoza, Yeats, the bawdy and wise,
Continuing their interminable debate,
With no conclusion, they conclude too late,
When their wisdom has fallen like a grey pall on my eyes.
Syne we maun part, there sall be nane remeid—
Unless my country is my pride, indeed,

Or I can make my town that homely fame
That Byron has, from boys in Carden Place,
Struggling home with books to midday dinner,
For whom he is not the romantic sinner,
The careless writer, the tormented face,
The hectoring bully or the noble fool,
But, just like Gordon or like Keith, a name:
A tall, proud statue at the Grammar School.

THE TRAVELLER HAS REGRETS

The traveller has regrets
For the receding shore
That with its many nets
Has caught, not to restore,
The white lights in the bay,
The blue lights on the hill,
Though night with many stars
May travel with him still,
But night has nought to say,
Only a colour and shape
Changing like cloth shaking,
A dancer with a cape
Whose dance is heart-breaking,
Night with its many stars
Can warn travellers
There's only time to kill
And nothing much to say:
But the blue lights on the hill,
The white lights in the bay
Told us the meal was laid
And that the bed was made
And that we could not stay.

ROBERT MACLELLAN

THE LANELY FISHER

By the wan watter o' the Fjallavatn
In the lang grey dim o' a simmer nicht,
There lie to the feet o' the lanely fisher
The bluid-bedagglet feathers o' the shalder,
The peckit banes o' the wee tammie-norie,
And daith's angel, the deil-faured skua
Twangs in the eerie glume aboot his heid
Like the fingert gut o' a boss fiddle,
Seeks in its lightnin' dive his thin-baned croun,
Its wud een lowin wi' the watter's licht,
Its forkit tail the fleein' skirts
O' a fang-tuthit troll; and at a likely rise
He lifts his heid in fricht, and jerks his flee,
The quick troot gowps in the toom air,
Strauchtens, hits the watter wi' a skelp,
And waukens the haill heich craigie quaich
Wi' the muckle black-back's bogle craik,
And the hairt-wrung wail o' the wheelin' whimbrel.

SANG

There's a reid lowe in yer cheek,
Mither, and a licht in yer ee,
And ye sing like the shuilfie in the slae,
But no' for me.

The man that cam' the day,
Mither, that ye ran to meet,
He drapt his gun and fondlet ye
And I was left to greet.

118

Ye served him kail frae the pat,
Mither, and meat frae the bane.
Ye brocht him cherries frae the gean,
And I gat haurdly ane.

And noo he lies in yer bed,
Mither, and the licht grows dim,
And the sang ye sing as ye hap me ower
Is meant for him.

WINTER IN THE FAROES

Deep in their stanie holes in the steilie burn
The stairvelin troots lie thin in frozen sleep,
Their toom wames worm-hames, and the hoodie craws,
At ilka yowe-hoast frae the snaw-smoored fank,
Tichten their quait, daurk, daithly ring
Together wi' black beak to the blank een
O' the first cauld corp, and flame and smeik
Belch in the heich craigs frae deidly muzzles
To scatter shot-stangs at the fleein' hares
That lowp and cowp and streitch, and stain the wraiths
Abune the grushie moul whaur the Iceland queen[1]
Sleeps in her seed by her deid simmer rutes.
The reid bluid seeps to her happit bed
To sloke her life-drouth at the sun's turn.
The eggs in the redds and the lambs in the ourie yowes
Bide their time tae, for pouthert snaw
Spumes frae the splintert tap o' the heichest scaur:
Daith's icy banner ower the haill isle world.

[1] KOENIGIA ISLANDICA, an annual peculiar to Iceland and the Faroes
which flowers above 2,000 feet.

NORMAN McCAIG

AT THE NARROW NECK OF THE LOCH

At the narrow neck of the loch, half loch, half river,
arriving when darkness felt first the drag of light,
half dark half day, we sat and watched in the stillness
gulls witlessly flitting along the narrow water.
Arriving there—or here—on the lip of change
what incorruptible silence
winnows our wings and locks the voice in our throats,

passing and passing. What terror and chain of unreason
slips us in silence, enchanted to its nature
so that we only see the twirling rise
or sideways diving of another's passion
repeating our actions in an untranslated
tongue of no echoes,
mirror of terror and mimicry of rapture

and cannot say or hear. And afterwards the menace
of silence is all we remember and the tingle and twitch
of nerves cursed dumb attempting to speak and sing,
and arriving there or here we sit, only with dull eyes
watching on a day half-scratched out of darkness
a dreary sea depositing
its doleful lumps of water on a dead beach.

NOW THIS WOOD OF ANGELS

Now this wood of angels, dolphin sighing in sea-loch
tingle in a morning light long in my level hand.
Steep aspens are motionless and between the birches
fall without a stir the threads of their branches
and the sky of morning lies level in my mind.

Across to you, away from the narrow ferry
leaving behind only for a mile's moment
the red sea-weed and the sliding blue of tide.
Leave sand to oyster-catchers for where only tread
otter and fox, or stag slots his hoof-print.

Between two ferries, two angel arms of sea
I heave this high headland over my heronry
berried with blaeberries and rounded with heather.
Eilean Glas my old sorrow down in the streaked water
floats away with it in a stripe of sky.

YOU WITHIN LOVE

You within love are lion leaping in darkness
glorifying night with a fiercer day,
passion of rivers leaping in curled dances,
greed of sun in all the whirling dew.
And love around you echoing only you
conjures the spring in the year's every day.
Bold sun, slim moon
that trembles beyond virgin
I creep with you behind the lion's pounces,
vanish in a morning glitter, rise with passion
in an echoing spring burn every day.

121

ALBATROSS

Now falls the bird where all the battle
of flacking oars spelters in the sea.
The glowing wings that wrestled three years away
crumple upon the brittle
and lazy diagrams of a bulging wave.
Fine drum-songs for his grave.

Bird no more blazing in my mind
I'll follow your hollow bones to the sea-foot.
I'll build you chambers of sand, I'll be sea's throat
and overcome of wind,
calling long choruses round the naked land
with combs of my long hand.

What wind will mutter in the double
desire of bright sun and lamenting moon
now that your slackened wings are folded down
and moused by a lipping ripple?
Wind's use is dead. But litanies of sand
will grow from my hollow hand.

THESE NORTHERN MUSICS

These northern musics twigging in my spring
call the rich dust back to their origin
in crumble heather leaves and bone gneiss.
The wind calls backward with a pipe of ice
to stone and bog
and leaping beaches where those green tides drag.

Further than chariot's dive with a roaring god
into his Erebus, deeper than the wood
with gold at heart and death in the evergreen
I plunged in winter with my Proserpine
and find still growing
top-heavy sea-pinks and the bull waves playing.

Winter my summer is in this dull winter
and snow winds blow a black and gurgling chanter
through the dull sighing of this southern wind.
In middle air a seal lies off a strand
dazzled with summer
and a green cliff rings with a cuckoo hammer.

Riding a twig, a cowslip sun, bee's back
outward from Dis, with no Eurydice look
to lock the swivel summer from my eye,
I take my quaver mistress on my tongue
and sing her over,
my lover music, I her singing lover.

TOM SCOTT

SEA-DIRGE

I found him drowned on the rock that night
And the wind high; moonlight it was
And the hungry sucking of the sea
At my feet, stretching away in front of me;
Never a lover was laid on the braes that night
Nor any living soul I'm thinking, unless they were mad
And drawn to the moon; I found him there
In the rocks that night and the wind was high;
Bare he was as the sea and the rock, on either side,
With a rag of silk in his hand
And sand in his nose; moonlight it was
And the sea before me: my hair dragged at my eyes.

I couldn't see, but a hand of ice was plunged
Deep in my womb; I found him lying
Drowned on the rock that night and
The wind was high; moonlight it was
And the sea sucked at my feet;
Then I heard from the cave behind
The skirl of the piper who died on rocks,
The wail of the pipes and then the cry of his soul;
I upped and screamed at the wind and the sea,
I stripped my forsaken breasts to the moon
And I kissed the frost of his mouth and the sand;
I found him drowned on the rock that night
And the wind high; moonlight it was
And the hungry sucking of the sea
At my feet and his clammy head in my breasts
That were bare as the rock and the sea and the sand

TO X

Not because your body is lovely or your hair,
Nor those wombs of light where love suffers openly
Nor only for the sphere our bodies make at night
Though these contribute, dear, and flow toward.

But because of the tears and our human needs
Because we met in the dark and bred a flame
That kindled in the ribs of each though never together
Fires that joined light across the seas that severed.

Because love is not ours to command or commend
But a wreath of fulfilment offering us
Ourselves through the gift of surrender:
Not to be coldly treated ever but made at home.

And because the heart mumbling over its isolation
rehearses death in desiring all its fears
Till love unlocks its tethered floods
Unfolding slowly the humble mother and compasses.

POEM

Out here on the sea I hear the wind and the night
Ruffle the hair of the dead, the beat
Of black wings among the stars
Hearing the dirl of ship and wave
Only hearing, hearing the snore of the sea;
The gurgle of ocean in drowned women is it, I hear
The wind or the wave or the night or the dead,
The dead who suck at my ears with the wind,
The eyeless priest and the gored nun
Sleeping deep in the slime of the tomb
Or the wail of a hanged monk
Over the rumble of wheels
In the bowels of the sea, the spiked
And spitted souls of children crying through the fog?
But here I am hearing the storm-wind sing in my bones
Meaning business, and I am glad, I am listening, listening—.

NIGHTSONG

The moon is high and at the full
And under that hypnotic gaze
Held in magical control
The world is frozen motionless;
Every star is in its place.

From her principality
Venus stoops behind the line
Of the horizon, quietly
As the deeper night sets in;
And stepping with a wayward grace

From her cave among the stars
Night herself plucks off her dress,
Slips from each silken thing that mars
Her beauty and her loveliness,
To tremble in the winds that press

Coldly on her drowsy skin.
And bold with desire comes stealthy up
And creeps unbidden naked in
To my empty breast, as in a cup
And cools wine's rousing kiss.

On my ribs her head's impressed;
Voluptuously her cold loins
Belly and her laden breast
Lie against my restless limbs
Drawing up a sea's distress

In one spear of desire; I am held
Thus, polarised, compressed,
But from that hymened echo exiled
Forever; held; the cold mist
Of the halfling world upon my face.

But held so delicately love
That if you come not presently
To prove this night, I fear the glove
Of mind will fall entirely from me
To rot among the silent grass.

MAURICE LINDSAY

JOHN KNOX

Who in his heart broke churches and burnt fugues,
walking across sprung heather in the sun,
darkness his head, his long gray beard like God's,
held virtue on an edge of ugliness,
stripped windows with a fanatic's delight,
raved bitter sermons to the baffled poor.

Who in his hand hurled an appalling Hell,
ground into atoms Grace beneath his staff,
hung preachers' plenty from his pulpit's pit,
brought stolid strength that stunned the source of love,
a fiery terror and the Lord of War!

JOCK, THE LAIRD'S BROTHER

Strutting across the red moors of his memory, Jock, the laird's
brother,
tingling, tweedy, bagpipe trousers, whisky map-veined face,
under his arm a leering gun, the image of his father,
the skirling traditions of fishes and pheasants, the ownership of
space;

the purple, peopleless moors of Scotland, where poverty snakes in
the ground,
and love turns grey as the ashy, prickled, bleak-burned,
skeletoned heather
where sleek guns splutter their patter in August, and gasping
grouse are found
on the noses of snuffling dogs, and the moors are always the talk
of weather.

O a health to the highborn, heartburn Highlands, where girls like
 retrievers, mate
for easy money, neighbours' fields, or preserving the brainless
 pride of the blood,
and the sneering world is weighed and found wanting in the scales
 with a shrinking estate,
and the poorer people are counted in stuffy kindness and solid
 food;

where the land is linked to its empty heads by custom's strings
 untied from sense,
and a cheap conceit, like the brightly coloured kilts of girls,
 makes swaggering play:
England, the decadent paper enemy glowering envy across
 the fence,
and the fists of imagination flourished against an advanceless
 reckoning day!

Once he was keeper of animals claimed from God to be owned by
 a Scottish lord,
once he patrolled the edges of forests, a poacher's pleasure his full
 despair,
now he is just the villagers' measure with his regular walks, an
 old man, absurd,
with the look of one who was left behind by his thoughts and is
 never here.

So it is with straining Scotland, jealous, exhausted, like a tired,
 fretting mother
she stares at her baby past and weeps for the lonely unhappy
 years that are over;
would she but change her thoughts, as the sky shifts clouds and
 seasons a little further,
she could be strong with the strength of all ages, and filled with
 the zeal of a laughing lover.

128

SERENADE IN WINTER
(for Joy)

Behind the curtain, shadows in the garden
gather, compress the last grey, wavering light;
black, lace-like patterns coalesce and harden
to uniform the drab and shapeless night.

Mud-splattered buses hurry home the weary,
fast, distant trains throw up a muffled roar.
White stars that glitter on the frozen Volga
are blotted in the Kelvin's foggy hoar.

Beside a muttering fire we lie together,
not speaking, Darling, on a soft divan;
and we forget the wars and winter weather
to learn the little happiness we can.

Watching your lips break into tenderness,
deep tides of love flood up your darkling eyes,
finding your face a map of gentleness
and all your supple gestures woman-wise,

oh, I am lost in vast immensities,
rich lands which only one explorer knows,
stretching beyond the sea-washed Hebrides
or where the unbridled Irrawaddy flows.

Like antennae, my drifting fingers fashion
fresh paths that trace the firm, instinctive bent
of Time's first-formed, exhilarating passion
whose fruit is life and ultimate content.

I see you as a warm and sunny harbour,
from battering storms a merciful release;
your hair, cool waters the tired hand would savour,
your breasts, sweet havens of desire and peace.

I see you as a maid in ancient story
whose beauty armed her knights with courage bold,
for whose fair name brave warriors gave tourney
to win a dearer look than royal gold.

Yet, where the fancy stirs, the spirit bends,
like rushes, swept and brushed upon a stream:
the heart still hungers for the natural ends
of flesh to build an age beyond the dream.

POEM AT CHRISTMAS
(to Joy)

To-night, a crisp air clings to the traveller's face,
sharpens quick diamonds set in city snow:
now, from this Northern land, I cross the space
between me and two thousand years ago;

where, in a stable, wind hustling the door,
a woman labours. Her distracted cries
startle the steamy oxen on the floor
staring at her with moist and curious eyes.

What puzzled thoughts were awkward Joseph's then,
hearing the cattle's hot, half-fetid breath
and the creaking rafters; seeing his Mary's pain
with more than ordinary fear and faith?

Did he picture stately processions through a crowd,
obeisance, jewels, the triumphant crown;
seasons and winds in their courses filled with the loud
glad truth that somehow the world would suddenly own?

Or was it all so much a personal thing—
how thin the straw that covered the cold, grey stone;
what it might do, this child his wife would bring
into the earth as his, that he'd not sown?

Likely his dreams were those of simple men,
hailing new birth to carry the sick years on,
learning always the need to begin again
as the long, slow candles of the breath burn down.

How could he guess, watching a lantern flame
flicker its quiet shadows on the wall,
stroking her hand, perhaps murmuring her name,
vast centuries would centre on that stall;

movements and peoples, churches, towers rise,
vaunt their vainglory for the gentle sake
of One who came with healing in his eyes
to fishers by a Galilean lake ;

that only His difficult birth could be wholly glad,
the world, as always, trundle its selfish way;
that a few would listen, but most would consider Him mad,
and all would deny His love at the end of the day?

As I reach in my fancy towards that far-away scene,
share the wild joy that to shepherds a white star brought,
oh, more than the earth's blind turning has come between
me and that wondrous babe three wise men sought,

more than clean time: the accretions of history
have piled their lumber on the accepting heart,
death's unjust litter clogged the mystery,
so that the mind no longer can see it apart

from the tragic human act; the unkempt fears
of poverty, lean hunger's cancerous ache,
the gash of unnatural loss, and the frozen tears
of wars that have broken pity over the rack.

To some, it is mostly an unbelievable story—
this sweet-faced Italian madonna in gold and blue,
a naked babe at her breast, in a halo of glory—
with a half-smothered hope that still it might all be true;

that over the newspaper's clamoured advance or retreat
the long-ago angels' *et in terra pax*
would fall as softly as snow on this Glasgow street
like sleep on a child, and the straining world relax.

To-night, as I turn to the Christmas-cracker glow,
the party songs, gay lights and the yellow sherry
pledging the usual toast that the ways we go
will be hedged with success, and all our days be merry,

my faith, like wine in a half-filled, uncorked bottle
has lost its taste, gone bitter and flat and thin,
and nothing I do will strengthen the flavour a little,
no gesture of mine can pour a new wine in.

So I watch the spectrum that plays on the delicate glass
you hold to the light, my Darling; and looking at you
I pray that whatever the future may bring to pass
that will hurt or please or maim, we may always be true

to ourselves and each other; to those who have suffered defeat
and are broken and weak, for whom love is an angry swan
its beauty shedded, hoarse terror cranning its beak,
attacking the cloud-white dream it once sailed upon.

For Love is the only faith that is certain and sure,
the only belief that follows no guideless star,
leading the vagrant heart to that stable door
and the symbolled birth no staleness can ever mar.

132

TO HUGH MACDIARMID

I

The English see you as an angry eagle
who tears at them with sharp and furious claws:
a mad, persuasive Gael who would inveigle
the Celts to raise their long-abandoned cause.

Sometimes they see you set in Highland weather,
red glens of shaggy cattle, a bleak moor
where game-birds flutter from the fading heather,
dark scented pinewoods laced with pointed spoor.

Or like the island clansman in the posters,
meeting the steamer once or twice a day;
or fishing with dour crofters for blue lobsters
to fill the creel-pots anchored in the bay.

They think that in your stern and rocky language
you catch the scudding Hebridean spray,
that words like sparks are only cast to furbish
the violent moods of Scottish history.

Your kilt, and all your gestures of romancing
are quaint; but oh! it's late into the day
to intercept the leisurely advancing
of England on her humanistic way.

And so they smile with unconcerned indulgence,
pay tribute to the temper of your thought,
admire your passion's vigorous effulgence,
but not the cause for which you lived and fought.

II

Only a Scot can know what you stand for, MacDiarmid,
a Scot who has felt the clear, bright Highland air
tauten his brain to a fine, resilient steel,

133

can follow the curve of your mind's incomparably rare
winged passages, and experience all you feel
of the Scottish earth's firm, sensuous tenderness.

Foreigners see our country veiled in romance,
a land where savages robbed and roved in clans;
our people, slow, unwilling to advance,
soft-spoken Gaelic ghillies, shooting hands
who labour to provide the Autumn sport
of English lairds, but never understand
the conscious English joke or the stock retort.

You have put that contemptuous nonsense back in its place,
and are no longer concerned with the rotting shielings
and the dreary, crumbling dust of a vanished race;
but with the steady hands and hearts that are willing
to cultivate the vast and desolate space
two hundred empty years have left behind,
you would cut all cancerous growth from the Scottish mind.

Like a lonely lighthouse perched on a splashing cape
that has felt the calm Atlantic glint in the sun,
or watched the impassioned, tossing waters rape
the thin, green fringe on the cliff in a furious storm,
you have looked on life, as it shakes its continuous shape,
with a strength which sweeps like a broad, revolving beam
on the tiny figures that creep on the heaving scene.

For you are not contained on the edge of an age,
easing the sharp, contemporary itch
with a trumped-up tag or a newly polished adage
for the anxious eyes that stare at their own last ditch;
but one who, on Time's lofty mountainside,
searches the clouds for where the heavens divide.

W. S. GRAHAM

MANY WITHOUT ELEGY

Many without elegy interpret a famous heart
Held with a searoped saviour to direct
The land. This morning moves aside
Sucking disaster and my bread
On the hooped fields of Eden's mountain
Over the crews of wrecked seagrain.

There they employ me. I rise to the weed that harps
More shipmark to capsizing, more to lament
Under the whitewashed quenched skerries
The washed-away dead. Hullo you mercies
Morning drowns tail and all and bells
Bubble up rigging as the saint falls.

Many dig deeper in joy and are shored with
A profit clasped in a furious swan-necked prow
To sail against spout of this monumental loss
That jibles with no great nobility its cause.
That I can gather, this parched offering
Of a dry hut out of wrong weeping.

Saying 'there's my bleached-in-tears opponent
Prone on his brothering bolster in the week
Of love for unbandaged unprayed for men.'
    Gone to no end but each man's own.
So far they are, creation's whole memory
Now never fears their death or day.

Many out of the shades project a heart
Famous for love and only what they are
To each self's landmark marked among
The dumb scenery of weeping.
I come in sight and duty of these
For food and fuel of a talking blaze.

Here as the morning moved my eyes achieve
Further through elegy. There is the dolphin
Reined with searopes stitching a heart
To swim through blight. No, I'll inherit
No keening in my mountain head or sea
Nor fret for few who die before I do.

O GENTLE QUEEN

O gentle queen of the afternoon
Wave the last orient of tears.
No daylight comet ever breaks
On so sweet an archipelago
As love on love.

The fundamental negress built
In a cloudy descant of the stars
Surveys no sorrow, invents no limits
Till laughter the watcher of accident
Sways off to God.

O gentle queen of the afternoon
The dawn is rescued dead and risen.
Promise, O bush of blushing joy,
No daylight comet ever breaks
On so sweet an archipelago
As love on love.

AT THAT BRIGHT CRY SET ON THE HEART'S HEADWATERS

At that bright cry set on the heart's head waters
I'm handed keys. I'm drifted well away.
Ahoy, shall I shout, emigrant to save me?
A packet of Irish returning to hoist the wars
rendering wherein the white world they trod.
Beside to sea I'm kindled by its garments.

At that cupped cry my kelp puffs up its hints,
Was mortal-caulked before it fell to the arrived
Contraries and kegs, bedlams of victorious vale.
And was before it fell to this formal ash
The manned quarters of my imagination's courage.
Bedside to earth and something of a man, I say
And hoist to words this arrival, and see sail
The deadly manroped hearties of a holy sea-vessel.

R. CROMBIE SAUNDERS

ABOVE THE FORMIDABLE TOMB

Above the formidable tomb
No angel will be known
And where Earth's child is buried, there
The void protects its own.

Spring had a smile of hyacinth
In the morning of the year,
Whose transitory innocence
Knows no revival here.

Her innocence could not foresee
That sullen death would give
To an ecstatic enemy
His own prerogative.

Below the lamentable cross
The weeping mother stands,
And love, for which her child had died,
Lies useless in her hands.

137

HAD I TWA HERTS

Had I twa herts an you but ane
 Whan we were twin'd, still for your sake
That I micht loe yet be alane
 Ae hert wud thrive, the ither break.

Had I twa tongues tae speak o thee
 I culdna let a morrow come
An hear na o your cheritie
 From ane—the ither wud be dumb.

Had I fower een an twa tae close
 Wi greetan o a hert forlorn,
The ither twa wud see a rose
 Ahint the gairden o your scorn.

But I am ane an sae maun find
 An answer tae the mysterie;
Dee an forget, or livan mind
 Aa times my troublit historie.

THE EMPTY GLEN

Time ticks away the centre of my pride
Emptying its glen of cattle, crops, and song,
Till its deserted headlands are alone
Familiar with the green uncaring tide.

What gave this land to gradual decay?
The rocky field where plovers make their nest
Now undisturbed had once the soil to raise
A happy people, but from day to day

The hamlets failed, the young men sought the towns,
Bewildered age looked from the cottage door
Upon the wreck of all they'd laboured for,
The rotting gate, the bracken on the downs;

And wondered if the future was so black
The children would have stayed but did not dare,
Who might, they hoped, be happy where they are.
And wondered, Are they ever coming back?

DONALD MACRAE

THE PTERODACTYL AND POWHATAN'S DAUGHTER

American poets have seen their country
as a brown girl lying serene in the sun,
as Powhatan's daughter with open thighs,
her belly a golden plain of wheat,
her breasts the firm and fecund hills,
each sinuous vein a river, and in each wrist
      the pulse of cataracts.

She has rejected no lover, not the
fanatic English nor the hungry Scot,
the trading Dutchman nor the industrious
continental peasant, used to oppression,
the patient stolen negro nor the
laborious Asiatic, schooled to diligent,
      ingenious labour.

By all her lovers she has been fruitful,
has multiplied all numbers, lying
indolent, calm and almost asleep,
only her lake-eyes watchful, expectant
of new wanderers from further shores
seeking her young immortal body,
      waiting unsated.

croons, emits a murmuring sound

cruach, heap, stack, mountain (Gaelic)

Daffan, joking, fooling

daurk, dark

daw, dawn

deemless, unjudging

deid, death, dead

deil-faured, favoured by the Devil

dern, hidden

dingan, driving

dings, drives

douce, sedate, sober

dounpitten, put down

dour, hard, severe

dree, endure

dreich, tedious, wearisome

droukit, drenched

dule, grief, sorrow

dullyart, of a dirty colour

dune, exhausted

dure, to abide, endure

dung, knocked

dwaiblie, infirm

dwaum, swoon

dwine, decline, dwindle

Eild, age

elbucks, elbows

eneuch, enough

Fank, sheep-cot or pen

fankled, entangled by means of knots

fash, bother, trouble

fecht, fight

fegs, faith (an oath)

feiman, in violent heat and commotion

ferlies, marvels

flaught, crowd

fleurs, flowers

flichtert, fluttered

flume, stream

forenicht, interval between twilight and bedtime

forfochten, exhausted

fowk, folk

frem, strange

frith, estuary

Gangrel. vagrant

gars, causes

gashant, prattling, gabbling

gausy, jolly

gean, wild cherry-tree

gentrice, gentleness

gesserant, metallically gleaming

gey, terrible (adj. or slang adverb)

ghaisties, ghosts

gin, if

girn, snare, grimace

glacks, passes

glaur, dirt

gleg, quick of perception

glister, lustre

glunch, to look sinister

gowd, gold

gowdie, golden jewel

gowk, cuckoo, foolish
gowl, angrily bark
gowps, gulps, gapes
graff, grave
greinan, yearning
greit, cry
gruntles, snouts
grushie, of thriving growth
goun, gown

Haill, whole
hairst, harvest
haliket, giddy, crazy
happit, wrapped
heich, high
heid, head
het, hot
hine, far off
hinny, honey
hive, haven
hoodie, hooded crow
houff, haunt
howdumbdeidsunsheen, sunshine at dead of night
howe, howie, hollow
hurdies, buttocks
hyne, few

Ilk, each
ilka, every

Jing-bang, everything
jizzen-bed, child-bed
jundied, rocked from side to side

Kail, colewart (used as a green vegetable)
keek, peep
kirk, church
kirkyairdielike, churchyardlike
kye, cows

Laich, hollow
laigh, low
laith, loathing
laithlie, loathsome
lauch, laugh
laverock, lark
lees, shelters
leuch, laughed
lift, firmament, sky
ligg, lie
linn, waterfall
linties, linnets
loon, fellow
lourd, dull
lowe, love, flame
lowin, flaming
lowps, leaps
love-lowe, flame of love
lozen, pane of glass
luely, softly
luft, firmament, sky
lush-raip, a blow that rips open

Machars, sea-meadows (Gaelic)
Mahoun, the Devil
mappamound, atlas
march, boundary
maun, must

143

mell, mix
mensefu, decent, sensible
merchless, boundless
mirk, darkness
mirkest, darkest
moujik, Russian peasant
mowdie, mole
mowdie-man, molecatcher
mowdie-worps, moles
muckle, great
müne, *muin*, *mune*, moon
murning, mourning

Neeps, turnips

Oe, grandchild
on-ding, fall of rain or snow
ony, any
oorie, chill, bleak
owre, over
owrecome, something that over-
  whelms one; refrain of song

Pat, pot
pechin, panting
peckit, struck
pleu, plough
poke, pocket, bag
pouthert, powdered
pree, taste, make proof of

Quaich, to scream wildly
quait, quiet

Rax, stretch
redds, clearances

reek, smoke
reeshlit, rustled
reid, red
rigg, ridge, furrow
roose, extol
rowin, rolling
rowtan, snoring
rutes, roots

Scaur, scar
skailan, dispersing
skailed, scattered
skaith, hurt
skau, ruin, destruction
skelp, blow, smack
skep, bee-hive made of twisted
  straw
skinklan, shining
slae, sloe
slee, crafty
smoory, covered with close,
  small rain
smored, smothered
sonsie, plump and good-
  natured
spaul, limb
speils, climbs
speired, inquired
steilie, steel
strampin, trampling
syne, since, ago, next

Tammie-norie, puffin
tattie-dulie, scare-crow
tattie-howk, lift potatoes
tenty, attentive

144

tene, sorrow
thirlit, pierced
thonder, yonder
thrawan, agony, death-throes
threeps, harangues
timm, empty
timmer, wooden
tint, lost
toom, empty
tramorts, corpses
trauchlit, fatigued, over-wrought
tyke, dog, loose fellow
tyned, lost

Ugsome, frightful
unco, strange, unknown, very

Vricht, carpenter

Wames, bellies, stomachs
wan, pale
wanchancy, dangerous, unlucky
warsslan, struggling
watergaw, indistinct rainbow
wauken, awake
waukrife, wakeful
wecht, weight
wechtit, weighed
weet, wet
weird, fate
weirdless, fateless

wersh, insipid
whaups, curlews
wheen, a number, quantity
wheep, to give a sharp, intermittent whistle
whelpikie, small dog, puppy
whiles, at times
whilk, which
whimbrel, a kind of curlew
whist, wheesht, be quiet
whusslit, whistled
widdreme, scene of chaotic confusion, sudden upset
wrack, vengeance, doom
wrack, whatever is thrown out by the sea; seaweed
wurd, worth
wud, mad, furious

Yalla, yellow
yammer, yawmer, whimper, whine
yird, earth
yirked, jerked
yowden-druft, snow driven by the wind
yowe-hoast, cough like a sick ewe's
yowe-trummle, cold spell at end of July after the sheep-shearing (ewe-tremble)

Exact translation into English is, for many words, impossible. It should be emphasised that, as with any other language, the translated version will rarely reproduce the atmosphere of the original.   M.L.